Your Divine Purpose

Discovering God's Plan for You

YOUR *Divine* PURPOSE

Discovering God's Plan for You

Richard Paul Anderson

Covenant Communications, Inc.

Cover image (top): *White Dove* © Christine Baldera courtesy of iStockphoto.

Cover design copyrighted 2008 by Covenant Communications, Inc.

Published by Covenant Communications, Inc.
American Fork, Utah

Printed in Canada
First Printing: January 2008

13 12 11 10 09 08 10 9 8 7 6 5 4 3 2 1

ISBN 978-1-59811-518-5
ISBN 1-59811-518-9

Table of Contents

Acknowledgments

Thanks need to go to many people, especially my wife, Susan, for her enduring support, insight, and suggestions. Thanks to my family for their encouragement to write and keep writing, and to Russell Springer for his keen eye. I had the privilege of teaching Book of Mormon and Doctrine and Covenants over a fifteen-year period at BYU, and so many of the religion faculty have influenced me and taught me much. People like Joseph McConkie, Robert Millet, Max Caldwell, Larry Dahl, and many others had an impact on my life that will never stop influencing all that I do, think, and feel. And thanks to the good people at Covenant for their wonderful help and enthusiastic support.

Introduction

Your Divine Purpose: Discovering God's Plan for You is a book for the ordinary, everyday Latter-day Saint. It is written for those who just want to do and be a little better, who sometimes feel they fall short, who are good people looking for that lost spark of enthusiasm and want an extra boost in being a disciple of Christ and a good member of Christ's Church.

Your Divine Purpose is designed to help put direction and purpose into your life. You are a unique and wonderful creation of God. When you align your vision and actions with God's unique purposes for your life, you learn how the most seemingly mundane acts can have rich and fulfilling consequences. You become more prepared to overcome your personal challenges. And best of all, you learn to clearly see God's hand in your life—how intimately He's involved in it, and how much He loves you.

In keeping with Joseph Smith's statement on self-government, "I teach them correct principles and they govern themselves," the focus of this book is on gospel principles with some stories to illustrate them. President Boyd K. Packer has taught that "true doctrine, understood, changes attitudes and behavior. The study of the doctrines of the gospel will improve behavior quicker than a study of behavior will improve behavior."[1]

Hopefully, this book will also help increase your understanding of how easily gospel doctrine can be applied to your everyday life. Life should be happy and fulfilling and you should feel satisfied with yours. Understanding God's plan for you will give such self-assurance. I hope you will read this little offering prayerfully and that it will provide you with the blessings it has brought to me in writing it.

Where Am I Headed?

In our bedroom hangs a painting by Derek Hegsted of a girl sitting at the feet of the Savior. As she leans her back against His side, one of His arms reaches around her shoulders and embraces her. His other hand is gently stroking her hair as a loving parent would a child. You cannot see His face, but you can sense the strength of His presence and the power of His love for her.

She is reaching up, holding onto His arm with one hand, the other hand tightly clutching His robe. It is obvious she wants to stay in the warmth and security of His love as long as she can. Her face expresses a look of contemplation as she seems to be pondering her imminent departure from her premortal life and His presence to a mortal life where His closeness will only be found by faith and righteousness. Though there is no fear in her eyes, and while it is obvious she has absolute faith in Him, there is a sense of apprehension in taking so big a step through the veil. But there is also an expression of faith in the image that is based on His reassuring promise that is the painting's title, *I Will Not Fail Thee.*

And this is His assurance to you. He has a plan for your life and it is uniquely yours. It was put in motion long before you came to Earth, and as it unfolds, it miraculously encompasses all of your premortal and mortal experiences. His plan allows for your weaknesses, challenges, failures and successes, and promises strength in the areas where you are lacking. It leads you on paths you would not expect to take, and brings people into your life you would not expect to meet.

Finding peace and contentment in life doesn't come by accident. These blessings aren't waiting around the corner for you to bump into them. They take work. It takes time and a conscious effort to align your life with God's plan. And once on the journey, there will always be course corrections, but He wants you to receive and take advantage of all He has promised. Consider these few scriptures of encouragement:

> Be of good cheer, and do not fear, for I the Lord am with you, and will stand by you (D&C 68:6).

> Behold, I will lead thee by my hand . . . and my power shall be over thee (Abr. 1:18).

> Be strong and of a good courage, fear not, nor be afraid . . . for the Lord thy God, he it is that doth go with thee; he will not fail thee, nor forsake thee (Deut. 31:6).

> Be of good cheer, for I will lead you along. The kingdom is yours and the blessings thereof are yours, and the riches of eternity are yours (D&C 78:18).

Will the journey be easy? The answer to that is yes and no. As Truman G. Madsen put it, "Is Christ's way a way of sacrifice, self-denial and discipline? Or is it a way of adventure, fulfillment and joy? The answer to both of these questions is yes."[2] And it is worth it.

Chapter 1
God's Plan vs. Your Plan

Trust in the Lord with all thine heart; and lean not unto thine own understanding.

In all thy ways acknowledge him, and he shall direct thy paths.

Be not wise in thine own eyes (Prov. 3:5–7).

It is a matter of trust. It is matter of letting go and acknowledging that a perfect plan for your life exists. Because when all is said and done, the value of your life will not be determined by your accomplishments, but by what your Heavenly Father has been able to accomplish through you. So it is a matter of trusting who is really in control, who your life belongs to, *who has purchased it.*

You have to let go and give your whole life to Him. Then all things are possible. "He that findeth his life shall lose it: and he that loseth his life for my sake shall find it" (Matt. 10:39). It seems contradictory that the fastest way to gain control of your life is to give the control away. But when you give your agency to the Lord, you will possess the greatest amount of agency. If you will quit misplacing all of your faith in yourself, you'll battle less of the accompanying self-doubt, because, as ironic as it may seem, you will have more faith in yourself when faith is rightly placed in the Lord.

When you learn of, trust in, and follow God's plan for your life, you discover a true sense of fulfillment. You realize that your life has great value, not just to the Lord, but to those around you, many whose identity might surprise you. When you know your life is in line with the Lord's wishes, you become content with yourself and accepting of those around you; you gain a clearer sense of your situation in life and what direction to take. You learn that many of the seemingly important things you stubbornly hang on to are not so critical after all. And when you finally let go of them, you feel a burden lifted.

Let what Paul wrote to the Colossians be a guide. You should "not cease to pray . . . that [you] *might be filled with the knowledge of his will in all wisdom and spiritual understanding*; that [you] might walk worthy of the Lord unto all pleasing, being fruitful in every good work, and increasing in the knowledge of God; Strengthened with all might, according to his glorious power, unto all patience and longsuffering with joyfulness" (Col. 1:9–11, emphasis added). These are great promises: leading a pleasing life; being fruitful; increasing in the knowledge of God; being strengthened by His glorious power; and receiving patience, longsuffering, and joy.

King Benjamin said you must become "as a child, submissive, meek, humble, patient, full of love, willing to submit to all things which the Lord seeth fit to inflict upon [you], even as a child doth submit to his father" (Mosiah 3:19). To trust is to be submissive. And as Elder Neal A. Maxwell said, "To be submissive 'even as a child doth submit to his Father' is a hard saying, but it is more than poetry; it reminds us of our true genealogy and our true possibility."[1]

Submissiveness comes much more easily when we humbly place our confidence in the Lord's ability to help and guide us rather than blindly finding our own way along paths of our own choosing. "I can do it myself" is a favorite thing for children to say to their parents. It shouldn't be one of your favorites with the Lord. Young children place trust in their parents as if parents were godlike, knowing everything, unable to fail or do wrong. Parents know, however, that they are fraught with weakness. God isn't. He knows all, will make no mistakes in guiding you, and will not fail.

There is no reason to fear or hesitate in "doing the will of God from the heart" (Eph. 6:6). Your submission must be total and your immersion complete. You can't hold back if you are to be "swallowed up in the will of the Father" (Mosiah 15:7). Elder Maxwell noted, "Most forms of holding back are rooted in pride or are prompted by the mistaken notion that somehow we are diminished by submission to God. Actually, the greater the submission, the greater the expansion! . . . It is the only surrender that is also a victory!"[2]

So the question is, are you ready to turn your life over to the Lord? You probably already know of many who have made this decision. There is a spiritual depth and strength in them, a peace about them. The scriptures are full of people who have made this choice. Nephi made it. So did Alma the younger. Peter did, as did Paul after his experience on the road to Damascus, as well as did Moses on Mount Sinai and Ether in the wilderness. Joseph Smith did prior to the First Vision, and so did Parley P. Pratt in Ohio, John Taylor in Canada, and Gordon B. Hinckley in England. You can undoubtedly add others to the list. The interesting thing is that they made the decision to submit their life to the Lord's will at different points in their lives and in a variety of different circumstances, each one unique to themselves. Their lives then took directions they never would have dreamed of, and blessings came they could not have comprehended beforehand. It will be no different for you.

Your life will no longer be subject to chance. Elder John A. Widtsoe once shared, "In my life's adventure, there has been no chance. Indeed, I doubt if chance has any place in a world supervised by a divine intelligence. Therefore, *I have felt that the power from the unseen world has ever been over me and directing my life's course*. That faith has removed both fear and dissatisfaction, enemies of mankind. Certainty comes to dwell when chance is removed. It has been easy to approach God in all my work."[3]

When you give something away, you no longer possess it. But when you give your life to the Lord, He gives it right back with so much more added to it. "I am come that [you] might have life, and that [you] might have it more abundantly" (John 10:10). Once you take the step, you will discover a new life and you will feel with a new heart. You will find increased freedom with your burdens lifted or, at the least, bearable. The Lord has promised that He will make your burdens light (see Mosiah 24:14). Such lifting cannot be found anywhere else.

God can do much more with your life than you can. Pray each day to be sensitive to the promptings the Holy Ghost will give you. Submit to the will of your Father in Heaven. Trust Him. His love and concern for you is unfailing. His plan is guaranteed.

Additional Scriptures to Study

2 Ne. 9:28
Alma 7:23
Hel. 3:35
Deut. 10:12–13
Prov. 3:5–7

Chapter 2
Your Premortal Foundation

> *We must not lose sight of the fact that the characteristics of the spirit, which were developed through many ages of a former existence, play a very important part in our progression through mortal life.*[1]
>
> *—Joseph F. Smith*

You do not come to this life empty-handed. You didn't enter mortality having to start from scratch. You were spiritually born of heavenly parents and brought with you heavenly characteristics. President Lorenzo Snow said:

> We believe that we are the offspring of our Father in heaven, and that we possess in our spiritual organizations the same capabilities, powers and faculties that our Father possesses, although in an infantile state. . . . We were born in the image of God our Father; He begat us like unto Himself. There is the nature of deity in the composition of our spiritual organization. In our spiritual birth, our Father transmitted to us the capabilities, powers and faculties which He possessed.[2]

What a wonderful thing to know! How often do you doubt your own capabilities when the real problem may be your failure to recognize and use them? No one knows how long his or her premortal life was. But think of the opportunities you had to learn and develop. Think of who your teachers possibly were. While there, you learned eternal principles and developed spiritual gifts and strengths. Elder Bruce R. McConkie said, "We are born here with the talents and capacities acquired there [and] the greatest and most important talent or capacity that any of the spirit children of the Father could gain is the talent of spirituality."[3]

In that part of your life, you were faithful to the principles you learned and to those who led you. Your spiritual strength was severely tested in the war in heaven, and you passed. As a member of Michael's army, you were able to help defeat Satan and his followers by the power of your testimony and by displaying such courage that you "loved not [your life] unto the death" (Rev. 12:11).

If you had the capacity to be strong and faithful there, you have the capacity to be so here. It wasn't lost at birth. The veil has kept you from knowing the status and strengths that were yours in the premortal world. However, your belonging to the House of Israel is a testimony that you were among a select number of spirit individuals who proved themselves exceptionally worthy, obedient, and valiant in their testimony. As a result, you became a member of the elect. Premortal Israel was, as Elder Melvin J. Ballard put it, "a group of souls tested, tried, and proven before they were born into the world. . . . Through this lineage were to come the true and tried souls that had demonstrated their righteousness in the spirit world before they came here."[4]

Mortality is the shortest but most difficult phase of your eternal progress. It is here that you face a kind of opposition not found anywhere else. President Joseph F. Smith makes this interesting observation:

> I think that [one's] spirit, before and after this probation, possesses greater facilities . . . for the acquisition of knowledge, than while manacled and shut up in the prison-house of mortality. Had we not known before we came the necessity of our coming, the importance of obtaining tabernacles, the glory to be achieved in posterity, the grand object to be attained by being tried and tested—weighed in the balance, in the exercise of the divine attributes, god-like powers and free agency with which we are endowed; whereby, after descending below all things, Christ-like, we might ascend above all things, and become like our Father, Mother and Elder Brother, Almighty and Eternal!—we never would have come.[5]

He continues:

> Can we know anything here that we did not know before we came? . . . I believe that our Savior is the ever-living example to all flesh in all these things. He no doubt possessed a foreknowledge of all the vicissitudes through which he would have to pass in the mortal tabernacle. . . . And yet, to accomplish the ultimatum of his previous existence, and consummate the grand and glorious object of his being, and the salvation of his infinite brotherhood, he had to come and take upon him flesh. He is our example. . . . If Christ knew beforehand, so did we. But in coming here, we forgot all, that

> our agency might be free indeed, to choose good or evil.[5]

You knew the risks and challenges of mortal life before you came. It is possible you knew who your parents would be and where you would be born, or that you knew the uniqueness of your individual challenges. Regardless, you knew it would not be easy, and, knowing all this beforehand, you still came. I think you came because of three things:

First, you believed in the promise of the Savior, that He would redeem you and not leave you "in a lost and in a fallen state" (1 Ne. 10:6). You had the promise of His help, and you had faith in that promise.

Secondly, coupled with your faith in the Savior's redeeming power, you had faith in your ability to meet the challenges you would face in mortality.

Third, you knew that whatever the challenges, it would be worth it. You were willing to put it all on the line, to go through whatever you had to, because in the end it would be worth it. Your divine inheritance, your spiritual genes, your experience through your premortal choices, and the knowledge you learned in that part of your existence all prepared you for this moment of life. You knew you would be up to the task, and you are.

President Brigham Young said:

> It is written of the Savior in the Bible that he descended below all things that he might ascend above all. Is it not so with every man? Certainly it is. It is fit then that we should descend below all things and come up gradually, and learn a little now and again, receive "line upon line, precept upon precept, here a little and there a little."[6]

So remember, you did not come helpless. You came endowed with and gained attributes that placed you in a unique classification of individuals. Elder Bruce R. McConkie stated that "Every living soul comes into this world with sufficient talent to believe and be saved, but the Lord's sheep, as a reward for their devotion when they dwelt in his presence, enjoy greater spiritual endowments than their fellows."[7]

In the premortal existence you lived in accordance with God's purpose for you. And here "all things work together for good to them that love God, to them who are called *according to his purpose*" (Rom. 8:28, emphasis added). By finding God's purpose for your life, you are continuing on the same path you were on in your premortal life and will continue on in the spirit world after this life. So as you tread through this life, remember you are not just fulfilling the purpose of your mortal existence, but also the eternal purpose of your creation.

As you align your life's mission with God's intentions for it, you will find your premortal attributes manifesting themselves in ways you never thought possible. And, as President John Taylor stated, "When truth shall touch the cords of your heart, they will vibrate; then intelligence shall illuminate your mind, and shed its lustre in your soul, and you shall begin to understand the things you once knew, but which had gone from you. You shall then begin to understand and know the object of your creation."[8]

Additional Scriptures to Study

D&C 46:8–12

D&C 138:56

Abr. 3:22–23

Chapter 3
Gaining Earthly Experience

> *The divine object of our coming to earth is to obtain a body of flesh and bones, to learn by the experiences which come to us in this mortal life the difference between good and evil, and to accomplish those things which the Lord commanded. Thus this life is the schoolroom of our journey through eternity.*[1]
>
> —*Howard W. Hunter*

Life is a continuum of experiences that prepare you for exaltation. How you react and what you learn from each experience is a reflection of your relationship with God. One of the secrets to aligning yourself with God's unique plan for your life is to embrace, learn from, and place life's experiences, good or bad, in the right perspective. Such perspective increases your understanding of how your experiences affect your relationship with God. A person can spend a lifetime asking the whys and what-ifs of an experience. But placing life's events in God's hands helps us keep an eternal perspective that gives meaning to even the most senseless experiences.

Without an eternal perspective, life's experiences would seem meaningless. We would come here, live, and then die for no purpose whatsoever. Joseph Smith said:

> It is important that we should understand the reasons and causes of our exposure to the vicissitudes of life and death, and the designs and purposes of God in our coming into the world, our sufferings here, and our departure hence. What is the object of our coming into existence, then dying and falling away, to be here no more? It is but reasonable to suppose that God would reveal something in reference to the matter, and it is a subject we ought to study more than any other. We ought to study it day and night, for the world is ignorant in reference to their true condition and relation. If we have any claim on our Heavenly Father for anything, it is for knowledge on this important subject. . . . Reading the experience of others, or the revelation given to *them,* can never give *us* a comprehensive view of our condition and true relation to God. Knowledge of these things can only be obtained by experience through the ordinances of God set forth for that purpose.[2]

Do you ever tell yourself, "I could do without this right now"? No one seeks for difficulties, and life is good when all is well with the world. But when all is well with the world, it may be a time when you are feeling, learning, and growing the least. The things that cause you the most inconvenience, the most fretting, the most pain are usually the ones that inspire your deepest ponderings and your greatest growth. Not placing these experiences in an eternal perspective denies you the opportunity of seeing God's hand in your life.

Many of your difficult experiences and unique challenges come from having a mortal body. Because of the introduction of sin into the temporal world, you are subject to temptations that relate to how you will treat and use your body. You must learn to control the appetites that come with the body, or they will control you (see chapter 20).

Your choices in this area affect the experiences you will have, either leading you to greater spiritual growth and preparing you for experiences in your next life, or robbing you of growth, causing a degeneration that can be both spiritual and physical. According to Elder Maxwell, learning to control the challenges of the mortal body will greatly increase our ability to learn and acquire Godly attributes—attributes that will be important after this life:

> It is especially helpful to remember also that the temptations and challenges we face are common to man (see 1 Cor. 10:3), yet we must respond uncommonly. It is also useful to ponder that fact that, along with even the Savior himself, we are to experience certain things "according to the flesh" (Alma 7:12) and to learn "in the process of time" (Moses 7:21). Built, therefore, into the seemingly ordinary experiences of life are opportunities for us to acquire such eternal attributes as love, mercy, meekness, patience, and submissiveness and to develop and sharpen such skills as how to communicate, motivate, delegate, and manage our time and talents and our thoughts in accordance with eternal priorities. These attributes . . . will be much needed in the next world.[3]

Other unique challenges come from our bodies having physical and/or mental limitations. The promise of the Resurrection takes on special significance in these instances. For those who have physical limitations, there are no boundaries for spiritual growth. For those with mental limitations, spiritual growth may not be as important for them as for those who serve them.

Accept mortal life and know that with mortality comes all types of experiences. Some may relate specifically to the mortal body, others to the spirit; and there is a relationship between the two where each affects the other. You're undoubtedly grateful for many of the experiences you enjoy. For those less pleasant, remember that you accepted the vicissitudes of life before you came. Having now jumped into the sea of life, you shouldn't complain about the temperature of the water. Better to see the distant shore and start swimming. Such actions will warm you.

Additional Scriptures to Study

Ps. 9:9–10
Rom. 5:1–5
D&C 58:2–6

Chapter 4
When Being Nothing Is Everything

> *For behold, if the knowledge of the goodness of God at this time has awakened you to a sense of your nothingness, and your worthless and fallen state—*
>
> *I say, that this is the man who receiveth salvation, through the atonement (Mosiah 4:5, 7).*

One thing necessary in learning to become submissive, meek, and humble is to realize the true nature of your stature as it compares to that of deity. Moses was shown this world from its beginning to the end, including a vision of all of God's children who would inhabit it. He saw God face-to-face, beholding the Lord in all His glory. Then he said, "Now, for this cause I know that man is nothing, which thing I never had supposed" (Moses 1:10).

Everyone has a need to feel important or needed in some way. You want your life to be worth something. But in the scriptures above, King Benjamin seems bent on ruining your self-esteem. He says you "cannot say that [you] are even as much as the dust of the earth" (Mosiah 2:25). On first reading, it would seem like you don't amount to much. But it is not a question of your worth. You were worth a world being created for you to dwell on.

The greatest price was paid for you to be able to continue living after this life in an exalted state. Your life, your physical body has been given to you. So what is the *nothing* King Benjamin is referring to? It is, as explicated by Joseph F. McConkie:

> The realization of [your] total dependence upon the power and blessings of heaven. [You] are as nothing in comparison to God. [You] have not even the power to make one hair white or black, let alone add a single cubit to [your] stature. Yet the miracle of man is the greatest evidence of God, for [you] have within [yourself] the power through the Atonement and the grace of God to become as he is.[1]

This dependence on God is reflected in the life of the Savior. Most actions He took were prefaced with prayer. He said, "The Son can do nothing of himself, but what he seeth the Father do" (John 5:19).

Moses was a simple shepherd living in exile in a barren and sparsely settled land. He struggled with his shortcomings. But by turning to the mount, he became one of greatest prophets who ever lived and whose works are referred to and remembered throughout the scriptures. Like Moses, it is eternally important that you "turn to the mount" to recognize you are powerless to accomplish anything without God's help. You are dependent on Him for everything. Each breath you take is because of Him (see Mosiah 2:21). Any blessings you enjoy are because of Him. Most importantly, you have no power to remove your sins, to save yourself from physical death, or to work miracles on your behalf.

In chapter 4 of Mosiah, the acknowledgment of your "nothingness" is one of six related things King Benjamin wants you to do. All six underscore your need to completely depend on the Lord. The six are:

1. Believe in God that He has all wisdom, and all power (v. 9).
2. Repent of your sins and forsake them (v. 10).
3. Retain in remembrance the greatness of God and your own nothingness (v. 11).
4. Humble yourself (v. 11).
5. Call upon the name of the Lord daily (v. 11).
6. Stand steadfast in your faith in the Savior (v. 11).

If you do these things, the promise is that you will have a mighty change of heart. And six blessings come with that change. You will:

1. Always rejoice (v. 12). You will find peace, contentment, and happiness regardless of your circumstances.
2. Be filled with the love of God (v. 12). Your relationships and love for others will become deeper and more meaningful.
3. Always retain a remission of your sins (v. 12). You will be free from guilt. You will feel accepted of the Lord, in spite of your shortcomings, and you will realize the great worth of your soul.
4. Grow in the knowledge of His glory (v. 12). You will come to know with more certainty the reality of His existence and the power of Christ's Atonement.
5. Grow in the knowledge of that which is just and true (v. 12). You will understand more

deeply the truths of the gospel, as well as discern other truths that pertain to your life and this world.

6. Live peaceably (v. 13). You will live more peaceably among your neighbors. Their faults will seem less important as you recognize the godliness that is in them.

Nothing does a better job of keeping you from understanding the principle of nothingness than pride. Pride places us in competition with others and even God—it places us in opposition to God and God's will. President Ezra Taft Benson noted:

> The central feature of pride is enmity—enmity toward God. . . . It is the power by which Satan wishes to reign over us. . . . Our will in competition to God's will allows desires, appetites, and passions to go unbridled. The proud cannot accept the authority of God giving direction to their lives. They pit their perceptions of truth against God's great knowledge, their abilities versus God's priesthood power, their accomplishments against His mighty works.[2]

Losing this pride and being totally dependent upon God will be reflected in your relationships with others. Consider how each of these passages have a common thread of humility and show implicit dependence on God:

> Verily I say unto you, Among them that are born of women there hath not risen a greater than John the Baptist: notwithstanding *he that is least in the*

> *kingdom of heaven is greater than he* (Matt. 11:11, emphasis added).

> And the King shall answer and say unto them, Verily I say unto you, *Inasmuch as ye have done it unto one of the least of these my brethren, ye have done it unto me* (Matt. 25:40, emphasis added).

> Whosoever shall receive this child in my name receiveth me: and whosoever shall receive me receiveth him that sent me: *for he that is least among you all, the same shall be great* (Luke 9:48, emphasis added).

> Whereof I was made a minister, according to the gift of the grace of God *given unto me by the effectual working of his power. Unto me, who am less than the least of all saints,* is this grace given, that I should preach among the Gentiles the unsearchable riches of Christ (Eph. 3:7–8, emphasis added).

> He that is ordained of God and sent forth, the same is appointed to be the greatest, *notwithstanding he is the least and the servant of all* (D&C 50:26, emphasis added).

By understanding your nothingness in relation to God, you open the door to every possibility of achievement and greatness. Rather than relying on your own abilities, which are nothing in comparison to those of God, rely on His power, which is limitless and miraculous. Without Him, you can do nothing. But with Him, all things are possible (see Luke 1:37).

Additional Scriptures to Study

Luke 1:37
John 15:5
Mosiah 4:11
Alma 26:12
Hel. 12:6
D&C 59:21

Chapter 5

At the Crossroads of Eternity

And behold, I tell you these things that ye may learn wisdom; that ye may learn that when ye are in the service of your fellow beings ye are only in the service of your God (Mosiah 2:17).

When you are living your life according to God's purposes, you will influence the lives of others for good, often having an eternal impact on their lives. Such living will also impact your own life in a similar way. The Lord usually answers prayers through other people, and He wants to place you at the crossroads of someone else's life. As your actions benefit those who receive your assistance, you come to understand the love of the Savior, His mercy, and His empathy.

Placing your life in the hands of the Master Planner makes it possible for you to be a part of fulfilling His plans. What a privilege! Sometimes you may make a small but critical difference. But sometimes your help may mean the difference between spiritual suffering or redemption, even life or death.

There are numerous examples of this in the scriptures, the greatest of course being the Savior, who placed Himself at the crossroads of every person's life through His Atonement and Resurrection. David was at Israel's crossroads when he faced Goliath and the Philistines. Jonathan, through his steadfast loyalty to David, saved David's life on several occasions. Esther risked her life by requesting an audience with the king (an illegal act punishable by death) to ask him to reverse a decree that legitimized the killing of Jews. Andrew C. Skinner gave the following insights about Esther's actions:

> If she kept silent . . . relief and deliverance would surely arise from another quarter. But just maybe, by refusing to act, Esther would be missing out on her foreordained mission. Perhaps Esther herself had been raised up by God for precisely that very moment for the specific purpose of bringing deliverance to an entire nation. In that comment is the great lesson that applies to each one of us at our particular moment in the history of the kingdom of God. Each of us must seriously consider Mordecai's question [to Esther]: "And who knoweth whether thou art come to the kingdom for such a time as this?" (Esther 4:14).[1]

Esther saved an entire nation at the risk of her own life. To commemorate this deliverance, the Feast of Purim was commenced by the Jews and is continued to this day. The Hebrew name for Esther, *Hadassah,* is used today to name various Jewish hospitals and relief organizations around the world. You might not be called to do something as spectacular as Esther, but out of the seemingly simplest efforts can come astounding results. President Hinckley once said this about missionary work, but it applies here also: "Well, we're all in this together. I want you to know that. I have a responsibility, and you have a responsibility. We each have a responsibility, and I come back to this thought: you never can foretell the consequences of what you do."

He continues with a personal example of being at someone's crossroads:

> I was riding a plane a few years ago from London to New York. I got into a conversation with a man and woman from England, and as a result of that little conversation, the mother and the three sons have joined the Church. Every one of those boys has been married in the temple. Those boys have now had sons of their own go on missions, and that conversation which I had on a plane will go on bearing fruit generation after generation after generation. . . . *You never can foretell the good you do when you become the means of bringing into the heart of a man or woman a testimony of the living reality of the Lord Jesus Christ.*[2]

Sometimes being at the crossroads has to do with temporal relief. Blessings will flow both ways. Important emotions will be felt that draw both parties closer to the Lord and to each other.

For example, the Relief Society president when I was bishop was a young woman with several young children. She was a stay-at-home mom, and her husband was finishing school and working to support the family. They were on a tight budget. One day, as she was coming home from her weekly trip to the grocery store, she felt impressed to stop at an apartment complex in the ward. Without a second thought, she climbed the stairs to the second floor and left all of her groceries at the door of a single sister. This sister had three children and had recently moved to the United States from a foreign country.

This single sister had just checked the cupboard and reconfirmed what she already knew; she was down to one can of soup. She was distraught and prayed for help to know how she could feed her children. She felt impressed to go the door, and there were the groceries that had just been left. The following Sunday, this sister sat across from me tearfully telling me about her miracle. I knew immediately it had been the Relief Society president. In speaking with this sensitive president, she admitted she was responsible for the sudden appearance of food. Interestingly, she hadn't given a thought to how her own family would get by that week. She had just known it was what the Lord had wanted her to do.

Examples of people being spiritual influences can be found in our everyday relationships and callings. Larry (not his real name) had been a bishop for two years and knew and loved the members of his ward. He was particularly concerned about one young man whose countenance was changing. One night, this bishop had a dream that was remarkably clear and detailed. In this dream, he saw the young man enter a bar, have some drinks, and subsequently commit a serious moral transgression.

The next Sunday, the bishop called the young man in. He asked him if what he had seen in his dream was true. The bishop was able to describe the young man's actions that night in such detail that the young man wept and acknowledged his sins. The bishop was able to guide the young man through the repentance process. The young man eventually married in the temple and is now active with a wonderful family.

The important factor in these examples is that the individuals involved were living their lives in such a way that they were sensitive to the Spirit. They found themselves in the right place at the right time and did the right thing. If you are distracted with other issues, consumed with your own concerns, or not living your life according to the Lord's plan, the opportunity to bless someone's life may be right in front of you and you won't perceive it. It will pass you by, and blessings, relationships, and experiences will be lost.

Doing even small things for others can have major consequences, for both the giver and the receiver. Doing the right thing when you are at the crossroads of another person's life is when your life will more closely emulate the life of the Savior. You become a savior on Mount Zion, similar to when you go to the temple and do vicarious work for the dead. When you reach those moments and have those opportunities, remind yourself that what you do now is for eternity. For "who knoweth whether thou art come to the kingdom for such a time as this?" (Esth. 4:14).

Additional Scriptures to Study

Gen. 45:5–8
Eph. 2:10
1 Jn. 3:23–24
1 Ne. 9:6

Chapter 6

Free to Choose, but Choosing to Be Free?

> *"I wear the chain I forged in life," replied the Ghost. "I made it link by link, and yard by yard; I girded it on of my own free will, and of my own free will I wore it."* [1]
>
> *—Charles Dickens*

A former high school friend once said to me, "I could never be a member of your church. I couldn't stand the restrictions of all your commandments. I wouldn't want to have a leader telling me what I can and can't do." What my friend didn't understand is that obedience to divine laws creates greater freedom, while disobedience brings a restriction of your freedom. "I, the Lord God, make you free, therefore ye are free indeed; and the law also maketh you free" (D&C 98:8).

Like my friends, as a young man, I couldn't wait to get out on my own, to make my own decisions instead of having my parents tell me what I could or could not do. I didn't want to have to consider the consequences of my actions; I just wanted the freedom to act in my own way. Of course, as I matured and gained experience, I discovered my parents had been right all along.

What I and my high school friend didn't realize in our youth was just what President Kimball counseled a wayward young man: "You probably think you have found a new freedom: to think wholly for yourself, to make wholly your own determinations, to criticize and decide for yourself what is right and wrong. That was decided eternities ago. Right and wrong are not determined by you or me. Those elements were decided for us before birth. We have the free agency to do the right or do the wrong, but who are we to alter those changeless things?"[2]

As the world becomes more steeped in permissiveness, the lines between right and wrong are being blurred to the point that almost any behavior can be rationalized. Satan is very active promoting his program to remove agency and replace it with his control. As you choose to do something wrong, you choose to have less agency. In the end, the loss of agency is the loss of ability to make decisions because you subjugate your choices to Satan. This is especially evident in the case of addiction, whether the addiction be to drugs, pornography, or sexual immorality.

This loss of agency is the complete opposite of the Lord's plan. He said to the Jews that believed on Him, "If ye continue in my word, then are ye my disciples indeed; And ye shall know the truth, and the truth shall make you free. . . . If the Son therefore shall make you free, ye shall be free indeed" (John 8:31–32, 36). The Jews doubted Him, claiming they weren't in bondage, thus questioning how they could be made free. "Jesus answered them, Verily, verily, I say unto you, Whosoever committeth sin is the servant of sin" (John 8:34). To be free from sin is the greatest form of freedom. Paul said, "Stand fast therefore in the liberty wherewith Christ hath made us free, and be not entangled again with the yoke of bondage" (Gal. 5:1).

Decisions that have a bearing on your salvation and exaltation come down to a choice between following the urgings of the flesh or the promptings of the Spirit. Following the Spirit brings freedom. Following the flesh brings limitations and lessens what you have to choose between. "This I say then, Walk in the Spirit, and ye shall not fulfil the lust of the flesh. For the flesh lusteth against the Spirit, and the Spirit against the flesh: and these are contrary the one to the other: *so that ye cannot do the things that ye would*" (Gal. 5:16–17, emphasis added).

Jacob put it this way: "Therefore, cheer up your hearts, and remember that ye are free to act for yourselves—to choose the way of everlasting death or the way of eternal life. Wherefore, my beloved brethren, reconcile yourselves to the will of God, and not to the will of the devil and the flesh; and remember, after ye are reconciled unto God, that it is only in and through the grace of God that ye are saved" (2 Ne. 10:23–24).

The Lord does not compel us to make any decision. Neither can the devil. "The devil could not compel mankind to do evil," said Joseph Smith. "All was voluntary. Those who resisted the Spirit of God would be liable to be led into temptation, and then the association of heaven would be withdrawn from those who refused to be made partakers of such great glory. God would not exert any compulsory means and the devil could not."[3]

The kind of life you live is a result of the choices you make. You make choices so often that sometimes you don't even realize you are making them. Many of them are incidental. Others are more critical. Small decisions lead to greater ones. For example, the simple decision to read the Book of Mormon can lead to conversion, if read sincerely (see Moro. 10:4–5), and this can lead to the major decision to be baptized.

When choosing not to follow God's purposes for your life, some degree of bondage results, depending on the importance of the choice. It's similar to being in a prison where you can only do, move, and interact as much as the prison allows. This is like spiritual death because agency no longer exists and growth is not possible. The scriptures refer to this control over mankind as our being grasped, encircled, or bound by chains.

The chains of Satan are also limitations placed on the mind, heart, and soul. Hardened hearts are always a result of Satan's captivity (see Alma 12:11). The ability to feel and discern things of the Spirit is reduced until all promptings are gone. You can't discern what isn't there, thus an eternal perspective is no longer accessible because discernment is left to human logic and is subject to the whims and limitations of the world. This captivity legitimizes sin and leaves you with the illusion that more freedom has been gained because you have exercised your free will to sin. This actually is no choice because you are left with only the ability to sin, and righteousness is no longer an option. Only when repentance is chosen can you be led out of captivity—and this is the great message of the Atonement.

Many of life's experiences come to you as the result of how others use their agency. You cannot control the consequences of how their choices and actions may affect you; you can only control how you react to them. But regardless of the circumstances and environment you live in, and regardless of the way other people treat you, you still have the choice to determine what you will or will not allow to influence your own thoughts, feelings, and behavior.

Many times the consequences of your choices will be different from what you anticipate. Regardless of how well you exercise your agency, God still controls the outcomes. He may grant the success you seek, but on the other hand, it may be denied for your own good. President Thomas S. Monson expounded on this principle:

> Often doors have closed before [you] that seemed to lead to the opportunities [you] thought [you] had to have. [You] may have assumed that the closed door was a reflection of some inadequacy in [yourself]; but perhaps the closed door had nothing to do with whether [you] were good or bad or capable or incompetent. Rather, even now

> a loving Father shapes [your] path according to a prearranged, premortal covenant; the opening or the closing of these various doors is dependent on the Lord's perfect perception of [your] developmental needs. . . . He says that he does nothing save it be for the benefit of the world (2 Ne. 26:24); he has promised that, if [you] will be faithful, all things will work together for [your] good in order that [you] may be conformed to the image of his Son (see Rom. 8:28–29).[4]

Choosing to be free means choosing the way of the Master. When your choices are based on following God's purposes for your life, you place yourself in a position to be guided and tutored by Him through a unique set of experiences and consequences He has designed specifically for you. He promises to make you a better person with a life filled with richer experiences and deeper feelings.

Additional Scriptures to Study

2 Ne. 2:27
Hel. 14:30
D&C 38:22
D&C 58:26–27
D&C 88:86

Chapter 7
Being Honest with Yourself

The just man walketh in his integrity: his children are blessed after him (Prov. 20:7).

Sitting across the desk from President Cox, I thought about how I had come to love and respect this man. He was not only a wonderful stake president; he was like a loving grandfather to all the members of his stake. You knew he cared about you. He had a way of making you feel that you were more important to him than anyone else, even though you knew everyone else probably felt the same way.

"Are you honest in your dealings with your fellow man?" he asked me. "I try to be," I said. Up to this point, I was feeling pretty confident about giving the right answers to the questions in my temple recommend interview.

Then he paused, looked at me for several seconds, and asked, "But are you honest with yourself?" *Wait a minute,* I thought, *This wasn't supposed to be the next question.* I wasn't ready for this one. I felt trapped. If I said no, did that mean I wasn't worthy of a recommend? If I said yes, was I being honest with myself?

As I struggled with how to answer, he smiled and gave me a look that kindly said, *Why don't you think about that for a while?*

I think about that question continually. I have tried to make it a measuring stick for myself, but it can be a hard question to answer at times. I have to admit there have been occasions when I've been stubborn and avoided the question in order to rationalize actions or words that could have been more appropriate.

In Shakespeare's *Hamlet,* Polonius accompanies his son Laertes to the dock. Laertes is about to board a ship that will take him to another land, to see the world and find his fortune. Polonius does not know when or if he will see his son again. And like a good father, he worries about how well he has taught his son to be strong and virtuous, to be wise in the world, and to be the kind of son a good father hopes his son will be. As the sailors call Laertes to board the ship, Polonius calls his son to him, gives him his blessing, and then imparts his last advice, "This above all: to thine own self be true, and it must follow, as the night the day, Thou canst not then be false to any man."[1]

In scriptural times, a man's word was his bond. Many important contracts were settled not by a signature, but by the promise of each person. Even criminals would rather face death than break their word. For an example of the strength of a man's word in ancient times, we can look to 1 Nephi. Zoram was a servant who undoubtedly preferred freedom over being someone's property, and finding himself held at swordpoint by a stronger Nephi, he naturally feared for his life. But when Nephi swore an oath that Zoram would be a free man if he came with them into the wilderness, Zoram "did take courage." Only moments before, he feared for his life and freedom. Now he made an oath with Nephi and his brothers placing them all on equal ground where each had no doubt of the others' integrity (see 1 Ne. 4:33–35).

The story of David and Bath-sheba is a tragic story of loss of integrity. David acted out numerous deceptions in trying to hide his sins with Bath-sheba and in arranging the death of her husband Uriah. What is sometimes overlooked in this story is the integrity of Uriah. When David learned that Bath-sheba was pregnant by him, he sent a message to Joab, the commander of his armies, instructing Joab to send Uriah to him. When Uriah returned, David visited with him about the progress of the war and the well-being of Joab. David instructed Uriah to go home, stay with his family, and sent a present of food to his house. All of this was a deception on the part of David. This is in stark contrast to Uriah, who, out of loyalty to Joab and his fellow soldiers, refused to return to his home and slept at the door of David, his king and commanding officer.

When David asked Uriah why he hadn't returned home, Uriah said: "The ark, and Israel, and Judah, abide in tents; and my lord Joab, and the servants of my lord, are encamped in the open fields; shall I then go into mine house, to eat and to drink, and to lie with my wife? as thou livest, and as thy soul liveth, I will not do this thing" (2 Sam. 11:11). David commanded him to stay two more days, even attempting to get him drunk, but Uriah still would not return to his house out of respect for his fellow soldiers. Uriah returned to honorably fight for his king and country, but the king he fought for deceived him and arranged for his death. What did Uriah gain for his integrity? What did David lose for his lack thereof? The eternal consequences must be considered. Uriah's integrity would be obviously recognized and rewarded by God. But David "hath fallen from his exaltation" (D&C 132:39).

In contrast to David, Job said, "All the while my breath is in me, and the spirit of God is in my nostrils; My lips shall not speak wickedness, nor my tongue utter deceit. God forbid that I should justify you: till I die I will not remove mine integrity from me" (Job 27:3–5). About these verses, President Howard W. Hunter said:

> How inspiring. Because of his strength, he had no concerns of the trivial temptations before which most people fall. Job had built into his own life a strength and satisfaction that Satan himself could not crash. It is also interesting to see how God was delighted with him: "There is none like him in the earth, a perfect and an upright man, one that feareth God, and escheweth evil and still he holdeth fast to his integrity" (Job 2:3).[2]

In making the decision to fulfill God's purposes for your life, it must include a decision to be honest with yourself, as well as with everyone else. President Hinckley said, "It is such a simple thing [to be honest] and yet so very difficult for so very many people. Great is the man, regardless of his other accomplishments, who is known as one of integrity, on whose word all can depend."[3] Joseph Smith urged the Saints to "be virtuous and pure; [to] be men of integrity and truth."[4] He said that he would "fellowship nothing in the church but virtue, integrity, and uprightness."[5]

Someone once said that integrity is best determined by your actions when you are alone. About this, President Howard W. Hunter commented:

> We should always remember that we are never alone. There is no act which is not observed; there is no word spoken which is not heard; there is no thought conceived in the mind of man which is not known to God. There is no way we can get beyond the point where we are not noticed. There is no darkness which can conceal the things which we do. We must think before we act.[6]

When you are honest with yourself, there will be no reticence in taking responsibility for your actions, words, or thoughts (see Alma 12:14). To maintain your integrity is of far more worth than any consequences you may face for not maintaining it. Taking responsibility for everything you think, say, and do will be a strong witness to others of your efforts to follow God's plan for your life. To possess integrity is to possess the love of the Savior, and He will say of you as He said of Hyrum Smith, "And again, verily I say unto you, blessed is my servant [your name]; for I, the Lord, love him [or her] because of the integrity of his [or her] heart, and because he [or she] loveth that which is right before me, saith the Lord" (D&C 124:15).

Additional Scriptures to Study

Alma 24:19
Alma 53:20–21
D&C 124:15
D&C 124:20
JS–H 1:25

Chapter 8

Leveraging Your God-given Weaknesses

> *And if men come unto me I will show unto them their weakness. I give unto men weakness that they may be humble; and my grace is sufficient for all men that humble themselves before me; for if they humble themselves before me, and have faith in me, then will I make weak things become strong unto them (Ether 12:27).*

God has given you weaknesses. He gives you challenges and allows you to have failures and shortcomings. He does this for a good reason. It humbles you and thus opens opportunities for growth. He also uses weakness to confound the mighty. He uses the weak things of the earth to accomplish His great works. He accomplishes this on a small or large scale, affecting one life or many. You may view weaknesses as a major hindrance in your life; the Savior views them as a tool for good.

On a Sabbath, Jesus and His disciples passed by a man who was blind. They must have stopped and asked him how long he had been blind, because in their discussion with the Savior afterward, they know the man had been blind from the time of his birth. Christ's disciples tried to determine whose fault the blindness was and asked the Savior if the man was blind from birth because he had sinned (in his premortal life), or if he was blind because his parents had sinned in this life. The Savior said, "Neither hath this man sinned, nor his parents: but that the works of God should be made manifest in him" (John 9:3). Then Jesus healed the man.

Moroni expressed fear that his weakness in writing the word of God would cause the scriptures to be ineffective: "When we write we behold our weakness, and stumble because of the placing of our words; and I fear lest the Gentiles shall mock at our words" (Ether 12:25). All men have weaknesses and fear the results of them. However, there are many reasons humans have weaknesses and many ways to obtain them. Poor choices, sin, and addictions are all weaknesses you bring upon yourself. These weaknesses need to be repented of, or they will slow your progress. Weaknesses can also be the result of the environment you were raised in, the amount of education you've had, your physical and emotional health, and so on. Then there are weaknesses that seem to be distinctly yours. You were born with them, and they are part of the unique nature that defines you. They are an ever-present part of your life.

You can repent of the weaknesses you have brought on yourself. Those brought on by environment and upbringing can be changed to strengths. Some weaknesses will be your "thorn in the flesh" (2 Cor. 12:7), and you may have to learn to live with them. You may try to ignore these, but they are still there and often rear their ugly heads at the most inappropriate times. They seem to limit your life and affect your opportunity for happiness. Others judge you because of them and even take satisfaction in the fact that you are less than perfect. But as Paul says in 2 Corinthians, these are given for the purpose of keeping you humble.

All of us feel inadequate at times. You just don't know if you're up to the task or if you can even deal with it anymore. Such feelings may be because of extraordinary physical, mental, or emotional burdens. Your capacity to cope, however, will be determined by your capacity to have faith in the Lord and acknowledge His hand in all things.

Before you were born, your innate weaknesses were taken into consideration as part of the Lord's plan for you. They have been given to you to fulfill the Lord's purposes. "I give unto men weakness that they may be humble . . . then will I make weak things become strong" (Ether 12:27). The acknowledgment of humility makes it possible for you to be successful in spite of your weakness—through the Lord's grace.

Such was the case with Moroni's writing ability. The Lord had no concerns whatsoever about how ineffective Moroni's writing would be. "Fools mock, but they shall mourn; and my grace is sufficient for the meek, that they shall take no advantage of your weakness" (Ether 12:26). The Lord doesn't seem to discount the presence of a weakness, but He promises it will not affect the success of Moroni's efforts. Then He tells Moroni that because he has acknowledged his weakness, he will be made strong in what really matters, and promises him he will yet sit "down in the place which I have prepared in the mansions of my Father" (Ether 12:37).

Weaknesses are a part of your life because the Lord wants you to trust Him. President Hunter explained this: "[The Lord] uses [your] weaknesses or infirmities to help [you] see him more clearly."[1] Humbly acknowledging your weaknesses to the Lord is how you reach out, take His hand, and make Him a partner in your endeavors. "Nevertheless, the Lord God showeth us our weakness that we may know that it is by his grace, and his great condescensions unto the children of men, that we have power to do these things" (Jacob 4:7).

Ultimately, trusting solely in yourself will never be enough. Sooner or later, you will need to turn to the Lord. According to Moroni, the Lord's formula is to (a) humble yourself, (b) acknowledge the weakness, (c) face your inability to deal with it without His help, and (d) have faith that the Lord will make you equal to the task. The Lord's promise in return is that He will turn your weaknesses into strength if you turn to Him. This may be a complete change from weakness to strength or, as in Moroni's case, the promise of success in spite of the weakness. Harvard theologian Peter Gomes made the following comments on success in spite of weaknesses:

> Put your confidence in something that works. It is God who will keep you when all else has failed you; and it is to God to whom you will turn when you have exhausted all of the alternatives. It is God on whom you will call when you get that fateful diagnosis; it is God on whom you will call when the bottom drops out; and it is God on whom you will call when you pass through those seasons of doubt and despair, when life itself seems not worth the living and you cannot remember the last victory; and it is God on whom you will call with your very last breath.[2]

President Kimball was continually humbled by his weaknesses but accomplished great things in spite of them. When President J. Reuben Clark called and informed Spencer W. Kimball that he had been chosen to fill a vacancy in the Quorum of the Twelve, President Kimball sank directly to the floor and replied, "Oh, Brother Clark! Not me? You don't mean me? There must be some mistake. . . . It seems so impossible. I am so weak and small and limited and incapable." Later that night, he "rolled and tossed and wept and walked the floor through the long hours that lengthened themselves out into an eternity."[3]

As an Apostle, President Kimball, who had lost most of his vocal chords to cancer, longed for the power to speak with the same eloquence as the other Apostles. On one occasion, he spoke to President Lee about this, and President Lee said, "Spencer, be yourself. Use the talents the Lord has given you."[4] Later President Kimball would say, "I still wonder what the Lord was thinking about, making a little country boy like me President of his Church, unless he knew that I didn't have any sense and would just keep on working."[5]

President Kimball became a beloved prophet, famous for his gift of work ("Just Do It" became one of his famous sayings), his ability to express his love to all he came in contact with, and for increasing the vision of missionary work in the Church to extend beyond the borders of the United States to the rest of the world. Following his death, a Church historian said this: "As a church historian I would put him with Joseph and Brigham. Perhaps one should not rank prophets, but he gave us visions. He let us see ourselves as a world church, including China, India, and the Soviet Union, the seven-eighths of mankind we'd largely ignored in our thinking."[6]

Everyone wrestles with weaknesses, failings, shortcomings, limitations, and being in environments they cannot control. Regardless of your situation, in some way and at some time, you will certainly fall short in this life. But falling short in the eternal sense will surely happen if you try to control the outcomes in your life without utilizing God's power. He will help. He "knoweth the weakness of man and how to succor them who are tempted" (D&C 62:1). Robert L. Millet provided this insight about his own experience with this inner struggle:

> Much of my own frustration over the years has come as a result of my refusal to let go and thus let God. Something—I suppose it is the natural

> man, the prideful self that automatically asserts its own agenda—drives me to want to do it myself. Oh, I believe in God, to be sure. I know that He loves me, that He sent His Son to Earth to help me. All too often, however, my actions have betrayed my limited orientation, my vision of Christ as a type of spiritual advisor, a sort of celestial cheerleader who stands on the sidelines and whispers encouragement, not the Lord God Omnipotent who came to Earth to make men and women into new creatures through empowering them to do what they could never do for themselves.[7]

In closing, notice the Lord's summation of the principle in section 1 of the Doctrine and Covenants:

> The weak things of the world shall come forth and break down the mighty and strong ones, that man should not counsel his fellow man, neither trust in the arm of flesh—
>
> Behold, I am God and have spoken it; these commandments are of me, and were given unto my servants in their weakness, after the manner of their language, that they might come to understanding.
>
> And inasmuch as they were humble they might be made strong, and blessed from on high, and receive knowledge from time to time (D&C 1:19, 24, 28).

Not looking at your weaknesses as stumbling blocks but as opportunities can remove a lot of frustration in life. Trust the Lord and allow Him to utilize them and turn them into strengths. You will have confidence to succeed regardless of your obstacles. This will bring power to your life to accomplish God's purposes for it.

Additional Scriptures to Study

1 Cor. 1:25–27
1 Ne. 19:6
Ether 12:37
D&C 38:14–15

Chapter 9
Knowing He Knows You

> *As important as knowing who we are is knowing* whose *we are.*[1]
>
> —*Chieko Okazaki*

The Lord knows the challenges you face in life, and He is the master problem-solver. Even now, whether you realize it or not, He is involved in your life in a most intimate way. He is constantly nudging you in the right direction. He brings you in contact with other people who will affect your life for good, and He is giving you experiences that are designed to bring you into a deeper relationship with Him. At age twenty-two, before I was a member of the Church, I found out God was aware of me long before I was aware of God.

It was about ten p.m. and I was on my way home from watching the planes land at Sky Harbor Airport in Phoenix. As I left the parking area and turned onto the road, I found myself behind a drunk driver who weaved from one side of the road to the other, hitting one shoulder only to cross over and hit the other. He narrowly missed telephone poles and forced oncoming cars off the road, some of them only missing disaster by inches. I knew something bad was going to happen, but I was helpless to do anything to stop him. I could only follow and wait, hoping that he ran into something where he would only hurt himself.

As we started to round a curve, I noticed a car along the side of the road. One person was standing by the trunk of the car and two people were kneeling down to change the left front tire. As the drunk driver came around the curve, his weaving took his car onto the shoulder of the road. The person by the trunk looked up just in time to dive out of the way, but the ones changing the tire never saw what was coming. He hit them and I knew they had to have been killed because the drunk driver was going over fifty miles an hour in a thirty-five zone.

I stopped my car and noticed a group of six or eight people springing into action. A boy about ten years old jumped in my car and said, "He didn't stop." I looked up and saw the drunk driver fleeing the scene. Since there were other people there, I pursued him, happy that I wouldn't have to see what I didn't want to see. I pulled up next to him at a stoplight on a freeway overpass and told him to pull over to the side of the road because he had just hit someone.

At that moment, the light turned green, and without looking, the drunk driver hit the gas pedal and slammed into the car in front of him. I pulled my car in back of the drunk driver's and put my front bumper against his back bumper pinning his car in. The man got out of his car and began trying to hide his liquor bottles in the trunk and underneath his car.

Standing on the overpass and hearing the sirens and seeing all of the flashing lights and flares in the distance was an eerie experience. My mind simply couldn't comprehend it all. I waited until the police finally came, then told them what I had seen. As I filled out the accident report, a policeman told me that two fifteen-year-old boys had been killed.

My big question was *why.* If there was a God, why would He have allowed this to happen? Why hadn't He let the drunk driver hit a telephone pole and kill himself? What purpose was there in life if it allowed this depraved person to live while the lives of two innocent boys were lost? It didn't make sense to me. At home, I sat in the dark living room and relived the experience over and over. Finally, in the early morning hours, with no answers to my questions coming, I gave up and went to bed. For the first time in many years, I knelt down and said a prayer: "God, if you're there, I would like to know if you're there, and I would like to know what the purpose of life is, because right now, it doesn't make any sense."

Two weeks later, I was in Chicago starting graduate school. My mind kept being drawn back to people I had known who were members of the LDS Church. They seemed to have something I didn't. Something in their lives gave them a peace I didn't have. I decided to look the Church up. I found a number in the phone book, and it wasn't long before the missionaries were teaching my roommate and me the lessons.

One night, after a somewhat intense discussion about prayer, we lay in our beds with the lights out, talking about what the missionaries had taught us. I remembered the prayer I had said the night of the accident and told my roommate about it. More to myself than to my roommate I said, "I wonder if this is an answer to that prayer?" The words were hardly out of my mouth when suddenly my heart burned with a wonderful warmth that quickly spread through my entire being. It was a physical and spiritual feeling all at the same time. I was awestruck. I couldn't say anything. There were no words in my vocabulary to describe the feeling. At that moment, I knew there was a God. I had no doubt He knew me personally and that He answered prayers. The next missionary lesson was on the purpose of life. What amazed me about that experience was that God had found *me.* I was just a kid, no one special. But God had heard me and answered what I had asked Him.

God is omniscient and knows you inside and out. He is aware of your every thought and every action. He knows and understands what you feel; He knows what you have been through, and He knows what lies ahead. He "knoweth all things, for all things are present before [His] eyes" (D&C 38:2). He told Moses, "All things are present with me, for I know them all" (Moses 1:6). Ammon described to King Lamoni that God was aware of him: "And Ammon said: Yea, and he looketh down upon all the children of men; and he knows all the thoughts and intents of the heart; for by his hand were they all created from the beginning" (Alma 18:32).

God also knows your problems and challenges. But more often than not, rather than personally intervene and let you know He is aware of you and your situation, He will use others to help you. Elder Atsuko is an example of this. Elder Atsuko spoke only Portuguese and entered the MTC early for a crash course in English. After two weeks of intense training, he joined a district of American elders going to Japan. English was a difficult language, but now to also learn Japanese was a formidable challenge. Without anyone to communicate with on a consistent basis, he felt alone and helpless. It was his dream to serve a mission, especially to Japan since he was of Japanese ancestry, but this was much, much harder than he had anticipated.

Elder Atsuko came from a poor family which was already supporting his older brother on a mission. He had one pair of well-worn shoes, one equally worn hand-me-down suit, one shirt and tie, no watch, and an old set of scriptures that someone had given him for his mission. Not long after coming to the MTC, his father died. He knew his family would now not be able to bear the cost of two missions without his father's income. He was sure he would have to return home. He was lonely, sad, and losing hope fast.

But the Lord knew who Elder Atsuko was and just what he needed. Christmas was coming, and the elders in Elder Atsuko's district put their heads together, prayed, and came up with a plan. After gathering what resources they had, they wrote to family and friends. On the first Sunday after Christmas, Elder Atsuko walked into sacrament meeting a new missionary. The miracle was evident to everyone by the beaming smile on his face. He wore a pair of new shoes; a new suit, shirt, and tie; a new watch; and carried a new set of scriptures. There were more clothes and supplies back in his room. And best of all, he would be able to complete his mission, because it was now paid for.

Carefully looking back on your life is one way to become more aware that God knows you. If you look back nonjudgmentally, that is, look back without assuming many things have been a coincidence, you will see events, people, and other means by which God has intervened in your behalf. If you look back carefully enough, you will see a pattern of how God has come into your life in just the right way and at just the right time.

We should take heed of this, for God has said, "All flesh is in mine hand" (D&C 61:6), and when we ignore His influence in our lives, He is disappointed. "And in nothing doth man offend God, or against none is his wrath kindled, save those who confess not his hand in all things" (D&C 59:21). Ingratitude is a serious sin and is an indication of pride and the desire to say, "I did it my way."

By doing it His way, your faith will increase as you come to understand how well He knows you. The Savior promised, "Draw near unto me and I will draw near unto you; seek me diligently and ye shall find me; ask, and ye shall receive; knock, and it shall be opened unto you" (D&C 88:63). As you draw closer to Him, you will become more aware of His presence in your life. He knows you from the top of your head to the bottom of your soles and into the deepest corners of your heart and soul, and He understands.

Joseph Smith noted the awesome power of God—a power that we can access just by seeking Him and by acknowledging His hand in all things:

> We admit that God is the great source and fountain from whence proceeds all good; that He is perfect intelligence, and that His wisdom is alone sufficient to govern and regulate the mighty creations and worlds which shine and blaze with such magnificence and splendor over our heads, as though touched with His finger and moved by His Almighty word . . . the heavens declare the glory of a God, and the firmament showeth His handiwork; and a moment's reflection is sufficient to teach every man of common intelligence, that all these are not the mere productions of *chance,* nor could they be supported by any power less than an Almigthy [sic] hand.[2]

You are God's greatest work and His greatest concern (see Moses 1:39). You can be sure that as well as He knows and governs the universe, He personally knows you and will guide your life, just as He so ably guides the rest of His creations. His hand is over all of His creations, and His fingers are intertwined with your life.

Additional Scriptures to Study

Jer. 1:5
John 10:14
Eph. 3:17–19
1 Ne. 17:13

Chapter 10
Directed by the Spirit

The Lord gives to many of us the still, small voice of revelation. It comes as vividly and strongly as though it were with a great sound. It comes to each man, according to his needs and faithfulness, for guidance in matters that pertain to his own life.[1]

—*Heber J. Grant*

Many gospel principles take a lifetime to learn. In this life, it is doubtful that we ever completely learn and understand everything about them and their importance. Some are more important than others, and utilizing the gift of the Holy Ghost is one of the most important. You may have the constant companionship of the Holy Ghost, but learning to recognize the promptings, learning to listen and feel when the Holy Ghost is speaking, and then following the promptings explicitly are skills that must be developed and practiced if you are to fulfill the purpose for which you have been placed on this earth.

The Lord will not leave you helpless to wander through life, guessing which direction to go in. He will guide you through your journey. Sometimes you will be quite aware of being directed; other times you will not. Consider just a few of the wonderful and varied promises listed in the Topical Guide under *Guidance, Divine* (emphasis added):

> Ps. 23:2 He *leadeth* me beside the still waters.
> Ps. 25:5 *Lead* me in thy truth, and teach me.
> Ps. 25:9 The meek will he *guide* in judgment.
> Isa. 58:11 The Lord shall *guide* thee continually.
> 2 Thes. 3:5 The Lord [will] *direct* your hearts into the love of God.
> 1 Ne. 4:6 I was *led* by the Spirit, not knowing beforehand.
> Alma 48:16 God would make it known . . . whither they should *go.*
> Ether 2:5 The Lord . . . gave *directions* whither they should travel.

In the early sections of the Doctrine and Covenants, you can see the Lord instructing Joseph Smith and others regarding the workings of the Spirit. Surely, many aspects of the way the Holy Ghost works were new to them. In section 5, the Lord says, "And behold, whosoever believeth on my words, them will *I visit with the manifestation of my Spirit*" (D&C 5:16, emphasis added). In D&C 8:2–3, He says, "Yea, behold, *I will tell you in your mind and in your heart,* by the Holy Ghost . . . *which shall dwell in your heart.* Now, behold, this is the spirit of revelation; behold, this is the spirit by which Moses brought the children of Israel through the Red Sea on dry ground" (emphasis added).

In section 11, the Lord instructs, "And now, verily, verily, I say unto thee, put your trust in that Spirit which *leadeth to do good*—yea, *to do justly, to walk humbly, to judge righteously;* and this is my Spirit. Verily, verily, I say unto you, *I will impart unto you of my Spirit, which shall enlighten your mind, which shall fill your soul with joy; And then shall ye know, or by this shall you know, all things whatsoever you desire of me,* which are pertaining unto things of righteousness, in faith believing in me that you shall receive (D&C 11:12–14, emphasis added).

There are four great lessons in sections 6 and 9 regarding divine guidance. In section 6, Oliver Cowdery has come to Harmony, Pennsylvania, to meet the Prophet, help him with the translation of the Book of Mormon, and learn if what he has been hearing about Joseph and the Book of Mormon is true. Before leaving the Palmyra area, Oliver prayed to know the truth of the whole matter, and through a revelation given to him through Joseph Smith, he learned four important lessons about being guided by the Spirit.

Lesson 1

If you are prayerful, the Lord will guide you by His Spirit, whether you are aware of it or not. In verse 14, the Lord tells Oliver that the reason he is in Pennsylvania is because the Lord led him there by the Spirit as a result of his prayers. The Lord tells him: "Verily, verily, I say unto thee, blessed art thou for what thou hast done; for thou hast inquired of me, and *behold, as often as thou hast inquired thou hast received instruction of my Spirit. If it had not been so, thou wouldst not have come to the place where thou art at this time*" (D&C 6:14, emphasis added). Because Oliver prayed, the Lord instructed him and brought him to Pennsylvania, even though he was unaware of the Lord's guidance at the time.

Lesson 2

As often as you inquire of the Lord in mighty prayer, sooner or later your mind will be enlightened. God knows the thoughts and intents of your heart; He understands how you feel and will lead you through all of your righteous endeavors. "Behold, thou knowest that thou hast inquired of me and *I did enlighten thy mind*; and now I tell thee these things that thou mayest know that thou hast been enlightened by the Spirit of truth; Yea, I tell thee, that thou mayest know that there is *none else save God that knowest thy thoughts and the intents of thy heart*" (D&C 6:15–16, emphasis added).

Lesson 3

In seeking guidance, one of the greatest answers you can receive is peace of mind. The Lord wants us to recognize this as an answer from Him. The Lord had given this to Oliver in answer to his prayer, and this was a witness to him that God had answered his prayer and that Joseph was a prophet, since Joseph would not have known that the Lord had spoken peace to Oliver's mind. "Verily, verily, I say unto you, if you desire a further witness, cast your mind upon the night that you cried unto me in your heart, that you might know concerning the truth of these things. *Did I not speak peace to your mind* concerning the matter? What greater witness can you have than from God?" (D&C 6:22–23, emphasis added).

Lesson 4

Section 9 contains one of the most insightful lessons on how to get an answer to your prayers. Also directed to Oliver Cowdery, this lesson explains that the Lord will not automatically answer a prayer unless you have thoroughly thought things through and then determined what you feel is the correct answer. An answer may be immediate. It will be confusion if it is wrong, or you will clearly know in your mind and feel in your heart that it is right. Most often, however, the answer will not be immediately forthcoming. Then, you must move forward in faith, trusting that the Lord will tell you if your decision is right or wrong at the appropriate time. If it is wrong, you will have those same feelings of confusion, perhaps even dread, concerning the matter.

Or, if it is right, it will be obvious; your mind will be clear and you will have peace in your heart and know without a doubt it is right.

He says, "Behold, you have not understood; you have supposed that I would give it unto you, when you took no thought save it was to ask me. But, behold, I say unto you, that you must study it out in your mind; then you must ask me if it be right, and if it is right I will cause that your bosom shall burn within you; therefore, you shall feel that it is right. But if it be not right you shall have no such feelings, but you shall have a stupor of thought that shall cause you to forget the thing which is wrong" (D&C 9:7–9).

In all of this, you must not fear. Three times in an earlier section, the Lords warns you not to fear. "Fear not to do good . . . for whatsoever ye sow, that shall ye also reap. . . . Fear not, little flock; do good; let earth and hell combine against you, for if ye are built upon my rock, they cannot prevail. . . . Look unto me in every thought; doubt not, fear not" (D&C 6:33–34, 36).

Elder Boyd K. Packer tells of an experience where he learned this principle as a General Authority:

> Shortly after I was called as a General Authority, I went to Elder Harold B. Lee for counsel. He listened very carefully to my problem and suggested that I see President David O. McKay. President McKay counseled me as to the direction I should go. I was very willing to be obedient but saw no way possible for me to do as he counseled me to do. I returned to Elder Lee and told him that I saw no way to move in the direction I was counseled to go. He said, "The trouble with you is you want to see the end from the beginning." I replied that I would like to see at least a step or two ahead. Then came the lesson of a

> lifetime: "You must learn to walk to the edge of the light, and then a few steps into the darkness; then the light will appear and show the way before you." Then he quoted these eighteen words from the Book of Mormon: "Dispute not because ye see not, for ye receive no witness until after the trial of your faith" [Ether 12:6]. . . . During the twenty-nine years following that experience, I have learned over and over again that all of us must walk by faith—near the edge of the light. Like Nephi, who said, "I was led by the Spirit, not knowing beforehand the things which I should do" (1 Nephi 4:6).[2]

I had this experience as a young bishop when I needed to call a new Relief Society president. I studied the ward list and asked the Lord to reveal to me who it should be. An answer didn't come. As the time approached for the outgoing president to move, I began to panic. A wise stake president taught me the principle above, telling me to discuss with my counselors who would be qualified, who would be blessed by the calling, and who would bless the lives of the sisters in the ward. He told me to decide on a sister and move forward. He said I would know if it was wrong, that the Lord would not let me make a major mistake. If it was right, a confirmation would come at the right time. I followed his instructions and came up with a name. I prayed about the name, but I could not get a distinct answer one way or the other. So I moved forward with calling and sustaining a wonderful sister. It wasn't until I laid my hands on her head and set her apart as the Relief Society president that the confirmation came, and this confirmation was repeated many times during the course of her service.

The accounts of Moses and the children of Israel being led through the wilderness, of Nephi and his family, of the brother of Jared and his people being led to the promised land are symbolic of the Lord guiding you through your life's journey. Utilizing the Spirit and allowing your life to be guided by the Lord will bring assurances that your life is fulfilling the divine purposes for which you were created.

The Lord wants you to learn and grow from the decisions you make. With important decisions, He will confirm that you have decided right and will warn you when you are wrong. He will grant you peace, enlighten your mind, and fill your soul with joy.

Remember these four lessons: (1) If you are prayerful, the Lord will guide you by His Spirit, whether you are aware of it or not. (2) As often as you inquire of the Lord, your mind will be enlightened. God knows the thoughts and intents of your heart; He understands how you feel and will lead you through all of your righteous endeavors. (3) One of the greatest answers you can receive is peace of mind. (4) Often, an answer will not be immediately given to you. You must move forward in faith, trusting that the Lord will tell you if it is right or wrong.

Additional Scriptures to Study
Ether 2:22–23; 3:4–6
D&C 78:18
D&C 112:10

Chapter 11
Self-Love and Self-Esteem

In order to experience true joy . . . at any time, at least three factors are needed. You need to feel good about the people with whom you live and work—your companions in life. You must feel good about yourself—not in any sense of conceit, but simply a proper esteem for yourself, well deserved. And possibly most important, you must feel good about your relation to God and sincerely love him.[1]

—*Russell M. Nelson*

Everyone hurts in some way. Sometimes this mortal existence can be a very painful experience. While it can be filled with happiness and joy, a healthy dose of difficulty comes with the territory. You have left an exalted state to live in a fallen one. You have left the presence of God to exist in a realm of spiritual death. Have you ever wondered how much your spirit stubbornly remembers but that the veil won't reveal? Or, how much of your frustration comes from being in a far less state of glory than the one you were previously in? In becoming mortal, you have become prone to sin and error. This creates guilt and an inclination to sell yourself short because of your failures and shortcomings while sometimes failing to see that everyone else is struggling in the same manner.

So here you are, with everyone else, in this mortal experience. Do you assume that anyone is getting by without major challenges? That would be naive. Everyone has to go through this segment of eternal growth. Since no one gets to "drop out of school," so to speak, you can be sure that everyone else suffers in some way too. Everyone feels inadequate to some degree, has some regret for misspoken words or bad choices, has taken a wrong turn down the wrong path, or wishes their actions could have been better. They just try to hide their inadequacies, thinking that it's not acceptable to have them.

In the words of Paul, "All have sinned, and come short of the glory of God" (Rom. 3:23). No exceptions. No escapes. It's mortality. It is the continuing saga of the strategic battle between the natural (fallen) man and the spiritual man, and the natural man seems to win more than he or she should. Since mortal life is in opposition to the life God leads, could this be one of the reasons why "the natural man is an enemy to God" (Mosiah 3:19)? If the natural man is an enemy to God, is the natural man your enemy too?

When you allow yourself to be measured by anything besides your relationship with God, you get discouraging results. Then, often you become defensive and needless energy is spent protecting your "turf" so that you can maintain self-esteem. Elder Maxwell tells us what this turf is:

> Just what is this "turf" we insist on defending almost at the slightest provocation? If it is real estate, this will not rise with us in the resurrection. If it is concern over the opinions [others hold] of us . . . there is only One opinion of us that really matters. Besides, the opinions of others will [merely] be

> lowered if we go on an ego tantrum. If "turf" is status, we should not be overly concerned with today's organizational charts. Who cares now about the pecking order in the Sanhedrin in 31 AD, though so many cared so much at the time? Where are those now who worried so much over losing their places in the synagogues? [2]

Measure yourself by the world's standards, and you will find yourself stumbling in one of two directions. One is faultfinding. Seeing the weakness of others has the uncomfortable effect of reminding you of your own shortcomings. The "natural" reaction is to be critical of others' shortcomings. You can do this by pointing out their faults to them. Doing this unrealistically shifts your focus away from your own faults. It also disregards the Lord's maxim of "with what judgment ye judge, ye shall be judged: and with what measure ye mete, it shall be measured to you again" (Matt. 7:2), by others as well as by the Lord.

The other direction you can stumble in is to be so focused on your own shortcomings that you fail to see similar challenges in the lives of everyone around you. This kind of comparing always leaves you perceiving yourself in a lesser position instead of fostering an equal and empathetic relationship with everyone around you.

In the quote introducing the principles of this section, Elder Russell M. Nelson pointed out three things that a person needs for healthy self-love or esteem. As he noted, the most important is your relationship with God.

When you understand that God loves you, the question of your own self-esteem and self-love fades in significance. It is replaced with a sense of your true worth and settles the unsettling questions you have about yourself. The worth of your soul "is great in the sight of God" (D&C 18:10) and to truly know that someone loved you enough to die for you is to know of your ultimate and eternal worth. The understanding of this worth is the key to how you should feel about yourself. It is not a question of self-worth; it is a question of the worth of the soul.

One thing that can seriously affect how you feel about yourself, and that is the most damaging to self-esteem, is sin. Sin allows the natural man to rule over your spirit and estranges or alienates you from God. The loss of the Spirit includes the loss of divine influence. The further you stray, the less you feel and the more you doubt. Conversely, the lack of sin allows the Holy Ghost to bring strivings to your soul that will remind and teach you how the Atonement is the true indication of your worth. There is something sustaining in the day-to-day companionship of the Holy Ghost. It prods you into a remembrance of your divine heritage, reconnects your spirit to Godly influences, and comforts and grants peace in times of turmoil. Sincere repentance is one of the greatest ways to build healthy self-esteem and self-love.

When you separate yourself from the world, you can see more clearly how temporal it is. The things the world values are seldom of any worth. The world's yardstick will always measure things woefully short. But when you use the Lord's yardstick, you learn that your worth is great, your purposes for being here are of incalculable importance, and your opportunities for eternal accomplishments are unlimited.

Additional Scriptures to Study

Ps. 8:4–9
John 3:16
Alma 24:14

Chapter 12
Purchased with a Price

We do not know, we cannot tell, no mortal mind can conceive the full import of what Christ did in Gethsemane. . . . We know he suffered, both body and spirit, more than it is possible for man to suffer. . . . We know that in some way, incomprehensible to us, his suffering satisfied the demands of justice, ransomed penitent souls from the pains and penalties of sin, and made mercy available to those who believe in his holy name. We know that he lay prostrate upon the ground as the pains and agonies of an infinite burden caused him to tremble and would that he might not drink the bitter cup.[1]

—Bruce R. McConkie

Gethsemane today seems a small place. Only a few of the ancient olive trees survive. There is a church and some quiet places to meditate or view the Temple Mount as the Savior must have done. The Mount of Olives was a place where the Savior was accustomed to going in order to pray and meditate (see Luke 22:39). It was on that mount that the greatest event in all eternity took place, the place where you were purchased. Every act of your life as a disciple of Christ comes into focus through that one event.

Gethsemane means "oil press" or "wine press," and the symbolism is significant. The olive tree was an important commodity in Israel. It became a symbol for Israel culturally, spiritually, and scripturally. The olive was an important part of their economy. A new olive tree needs great care for it to bring forth its fruit. Once established, the olive tree is considered immortal because it can live for extremely long periods of time. Ancient roots that seem dead can still bring forth new growth. In Gethsemane today, there are roots of olive trees that may be old enough to have existed at the time of Christ.

When the olive is harvested, it is taken to the olive press. At the time of the Savior, these presses used wheel-like stones to crush the olives. Some of these stones were heavy enough that they needed to be moved by large beasts of burden. Only through the pressure of that weight was the oil removed from the fruit and its seed. The oil was an important source of Israel's commerce and was a part of many aspects of their life. It was their source of light. It was used medicinally for healing purposes.

Because of its purity, it was used for sacred rituals in their temple. And because of its purity and symbolic characteristics, we use it in our sacred ordinances in the Church and temple today. In Gethsemane, the Savior was subjected to such pressure that He sweat great drops of blood, and it is by this "oil" that you are healed. The Savior is your never-failing source of light and to whom you can go for constant nourishment. Symbolically, you partake of the fruit of this press each week. And it can be the source of great spiritual transformation.

Alma states, "The Son of God suffereth according to the flesh that he might take upon him the sins of his people, that he might blot out their transgressions according to the power of his deliverance" (Alma 7:13). There is no greater burden than sin. When the Savior bore the weight of all the world's guilt and ills upon His shoulders, He was pure, holy, and perfect in every moral and spiritual aspect of His life. He knew what guilt was—though He had never sinned, He felt it.

It is impossible to imagine how He must have felt as He assumed responsibility for the filthiness and guilt for all sins, from the smallest to the most heinous. The absence of sin had enabled Him to enjoy an intimate closeness with the Father, a closeness He would now lose because He had "trodden the wine-press alone" (D&C 76:107). God cannot abide with sin "with the least degree of allowance" (Alma 45:16), and now the Son was steeped in all of the sins of the world; thus the Father withdrew His presence from the Son. Of this event, Robert Millet wrote:

> There was a tragic aura surrounding this night of nights, when he who had always pleased the Father (John 8:29) and had thus never been alone (so far as being separated spiritually from his Father was concerned) was subjected to the forces and effects of sin that he had never known, forces that must have been poignantly and excruciatingly intense. . . . [He] knew all things . . . and yet there was something he had never known personally: he had known neither sin nor its effects. . . . This was a night of irony. He who was sinless became, as it were, the great sinner. . . . He who deserved least of all to suffer, now suffered most—more than mortal mind can fathom. He who had brought life . . . was subjected to the powers of death and darkness. [2]

Elder Maxwell approached the experience of Christ's suffering by examining the intimate language used in scripture:

> Jesus began to be "sore amazed" (Mark 14:33), or, in the Greek, "awestruck" and "astonished." . . . Jesus knew cognitively what He must do, but not experientially. He had never personally known the exquisite and exacting process of an atonement before. Thus, when the agony came in its fulness, it was . . . worse than even He with his unique intellect had ever imagined![3]

We get a small idea of the Savior's suffering by looking at how one person, Alma, suffered for his sins. The Book of Mormon says that Alma, along with the sons of Mosiah, was the "very vilest of sinners" (Mosiah 28:4). In what must have been a deeply personal and poignant conversation, Alma described to his son Helaman his suffering for the guilt of his sins in Alma chapter 36 (verses 11–17, emphasis added). Look at the words he uses to describe how he felt:

> He was "*struck* with . . . great *fear* and *amazement*" (v. 11).
> His "soul was *harrowed* up to the greatest degree and *racked* with all [his] sins" (v. 12).
> He was "*tormented* with the *pains* of hell" (v. 13).
> His soul was besieged by "*inexpressible horror*" (v. 14).
> He was "*racked*, even with the *pains* of a damned soul" (v. 16).
> He was "*harrowed* up by the memory of [his] many sins" (v. 17).

The word *harrowed* means distressed, afflicted, grieved, tormented, pained, mortified.

It is interesting to note that Alma says that when he had repented, his "soul was filled with joy as exceeding as was [his] pain" that "there [could] be nothing so exquisite and sweet as was [his] joy" (Alma 36:20–21).

Alma's experience with the weight of his own sins would give him a certain understanding of what the Savior suffered. In describing the Savior's suffering, he pointed out that added to the weight of sin and guilt was the suffering for the pains and illnesses associated with this life. Alma declared:

> And he shall go forth, suffering pains and afflictions and temptations of every kind; and this that the word might be fulfilled which saith he will take upon him the pains and the sicknesses of his people. . . .
>
> And he will take upon him their infirmities, that his bowels may be filled with mercy, according to the flesh, that he may know according to the flesh how to succor [care for] his people according to their infirmities (Alma 7:11–12).

When you think of all the possible ways a person can suffer in this life, be it from physical illness, pain and injury, or emotional and psychological trauma, the manner in which the Savior suffered is incomprehensible. And yet, He did this that He might know exactly how you would feel in your circumstances. With that knowledge, He would know how to care for you perfectly and see you through whatever the trial might be.

And He didn't suffer at the same level you or I would and go no further; He "descended below all things, in that he comprehended all things, that he might be in all and through all things" (D&C 88:6). In other words, He suffered beyond what you might suffer so that nothing would be unknown to Him. This, in part, is why the angel told Nephi to "Look and behold the condescension of God!" (1 Ne. 11:26) and why Jacob exclaimed, "O how great the holiness of our God! For he knoweth all things, and there is not anything save he knows it. And he cometh into the world that he may save all men if they will hearken unto his voice; for behold, *he suffereth the pains of all men, yea, the pains of every living creature, both men, women, and children, who belong to the family of Adam*" (2 Ne. 9:20–21, emphasis added).

About His own suffering, the Savior said it "caused myself, even God, the greatest of all, to tremble because of pain, and to bleed at every pore, and to suffer both body and spirit—and would that I might not drink the bitter cup, and shrink" (D&C 19:18). And, as the scriptures say, for all this, "He is despised and rejected of men; a man of sorrows, and acquainted with grief. . . . Surely he hath borne [your] griefs, and carried [your] sorrows: yet we did esteem him stricken, smitten of God, and afflicted. But he was wounded for [your] transgressions, he was bruised for [your] iniquities: the chastisement of [your] peace was upon him; and with his stripes [you] are healed" (Isa. 53:3–5).

Elder Neal A. Maxwell said:

> Can we, even in the depths of disease, tell Him anything at all about suffering? In ways we cannot comprehend, our sicknesses and infirmities were borne by Him even before they were borne by us. The very weight of our combined sins caused Him to descend below all. We have never been, nor will we be, in depths such as He has known.

> Thus His atonement made perfect His empathy and His mercy and His capacity to succor us, for which we can be everlastingly grateful as He tutors us in our trials.[4]

You have been purchased with a great price. Paul says, "Ye are bought with a price" (1 Cor. 6:20), and Peter says, "Ye know that ye were not redeemed with corruptible things, as silver and gold . . . But with the precious blood of Christ" (1 Pet. 1:18–19). Those who love Him and worship Him, who repent and turn their lives over to Him, are those of whom Abinadi says, "For these are they whose sins he has borne; these are they for whom he has died, to redeem them from their transgressions" (Mosiah 15:12).

To love Christ, to love His gospel, to appreciate His sacrifice, you must emulate Him by subjecting your will to the Father's. With such a great price paid in your behalf, you should do as Ammon and fall to your knees and pour out your soul in "prayer and thanksgiving to God for what he had done" (Alma 19:14). As Moroni says:

> Come unto Christ, and be perfected in him, and deny yourselves of all ungodliness; and if ye shall deny yourselves of all ungodliness, and love God with all your might, mind and strength, then is his grace sufficient for you, that by his grace ye may be perfect in Christ; and if by the grace of God ye are perfect in Christ, ye can in nowise deny the power of God.
>
> And again, if ye by the grace of God are perfect in Christ, and deny not his power, then are ye sanctified in Christ by the grace of God, through the

> shedding of the blood of Christ, which is in the covenant of the Father unto the remission of your sins, that ye become holy, without spot (Moro. 10:32–33).

Additional Scriptures to Study

Mosiah 3:7–9
Mosiah 4:6–7
Mosiah 15:7–9
Alma 23:24

Chapter 13

The Lifting Principle

Cause me to hear thy lovingkindness in the morning; for in thee do I trust: cause me to know the way wherein I should walk; for I lift up my soul unto thee (Ps. 143:8).

Humble yourselves in the sight of the Lord, and he shall lift you up (James 4:10).

And he said unto them, What man shall there be among you, that shall have one sheep, and if it fall into a pit on the sabbath day, will he not lay hold on it, and lift it out? (Matt. 12:11).

The scriptures above refer to the three aspects of the "lifting principle," all of which are interrelated. First, you lift your soul to Christ. As you do this, He will lift you. You are then in a position of being able to lift others. The beauty of the principle is, the more you do one, the more the others can consequently take place. For example, the more you lift others, the more you lift your soul to Christ, and the more you feel lifted by Him.

"Rejoice the soul of thy servant: for unto thee, O Lord, do I lift up my soul" (Ps. 86:4). In the scriptures, this takes on several meanings. It can mean turning to Him in prayer, to righteousness, or turning your heart to Him. You think of Him throughout the day. You couch your actions in His will. When you do this, you well be led, like Nephi, to say, "Behold, my soul delighteth in the things of the Lord; and my heart pondereth continually upon the things which I have seen and heard" (2 Ne. 4:16).

Like everyone else, you fight the battle between who you are and who you know you should be. Nephi knew he was mortal and recognized the battle between his soul and the weaknesses that come with mortality. "My heart sorroweth because of my flesh; my soul grieveth because of mine iniquities. I am encompassed about, because of the temptations and the sins which do so easily beset me. And when I desire to rejoice, my heart groaneth because of my sins." The next sentence is the key: "Nevertheless, I know in whom I have trusted" (2 Ne. 4:17–19). Verse 30 of the same chapter tells us where Nephi's heart and soul are: "Rejoice, O my heart, and cry unto the Lord, and say: O Lord, I will praise thee forever; yea, my soul will rejoice in thee, my God, and the rock of my salvation." By lifting your soul to God, you recognize your dependence upon Him and thus can have Him lift you through your faith.

The second aspect of the "lifting principle" is your need to be lifted by God. You can change your focus and actions, but when it comes to spiritual matters, only Christ can lift you to a higher level. James says, "Humble yourselves in the sight of the Lord, and he shall lift you up" (James 4:10). Oliver Cowdery's brother Warren received this same promise directly from the Lord: "Therefore, blessed is my servant Warren, for I will have mercy on him; and, notwithstanding the vanity of his heart, I will lift him up inasmuch as he will humble himself before me" (D&C 106:7).

God can lift you from a sinful state to a state of forgiveness and cleanliness. He says, "And as many as have received me, to them have I given to become the sons of God . . . for behold, by me redemption cometh" (3 Ne. 9:17; see also 2 Ne. 2:6). The Savior taught the Nephites, "And my Father sent me that I might be lifted up upon the cross; and after that I had been lifted up upon the cross, that I might draw all men unto me, that as I have been lifted up by men even so should men be lifted up by the Father" (3 Ne. 27:14).

Of this idea, Elder Richard G. Scott said, "I cannot comprehend his power, his majesty, his perfections. But I do understand something of his love, his compassion, his mercy. There is no burden he cannot lift. There is no heart he cannot purify and fill with joy. There is no life he cannot cleanse and restore when one is obedient to his teachings."[1]

God can lift you to higher levels of knowledge and revelation. The promise is, as you receive truth and live by it, you will receive more. As Isaiah states, it will come a step at a time, for "precept must be upon precept . . . line upon line . . . here a little, and there a little" (Isa. 28:10). In contending with Zeezrom and his worldly wisdom, Alma stated, "And he that will not harden his heart, to him is given the greater portion of the word, until it is given unto him to know the mysteries of God until he know them in full" (Alma 12:10). And lastly, the Lord told Joseph Smith, "That which is of God is light; and he that receiveth light, and continueth in God, receiveth more light; and that light groweth brighter and brighter until the perfect day" (D&C 50:24).

Two very important ways in which the Lord lifts you is through resurrection and redemption from death, and through exaltation. In his poignant last messages to his son Moroni, Mormon counseled his son, saying, "My son, be faithful in Christ; and may not the things which I have written grieve thee, to weigh thee down unto death; but may Christ lift thee up, and may his sufferings and death, and the showing his body unto our fathers, and his mercy and long-suffering, and the hope of his glory and of eternal life, rest in your mind forever" (Moro. 9:25).

Along these lines, Nephi prays, "Wherefore, may God raise you from death by the power of the resurrection, and also from everlasting death by the power of the atonement, that ye may be received into the eternal kingdom of God, that ye may praise him through grace divine" (2 Ne. 10:25).

The third facet of the lifting principle is your lifting of others. The parable of the good Samaritan (see Luke 10:30–37) focuses on the need to humbly offer aid to another, to lift them to something better regardless of their circumstances. The Savior expects you to assist Him in bringing about healing and comfort to the lives of others.

> And a certain man lame from his mother's womb was carried, whom they laid daily at the gate of the temple which is called Beautiful, to ask alms of them that entered into the temple;
>
> Who seeing Peter and John about to go into the temple asked an alms.
>
> And Peter, fastening his eyes upon him with John, said, Look on us.
>
> And he gave heed unto them, expecting to receive something of them.
>
> Then Peter said, Silver and gold have I none; but such as I have give I thee: In the name of Jesus Christ of Nazareth rise up and walk.

> And he took him by the right hand, and lifted him up: and immediately his feet and ankle bones received strength.
>
> And he leaping up stood, and walked, and entered with them into the temple, walking, and leaping, and praising God (Acts 3:2–8).

President Gordon B. Hinckley commented on this instance of lifting: "Now note that Peter took him by the right hand and lifted him up. Peter had to reach down to lift the lame man. We must also reach down."[2]

A more contemporary example of lifting and healing is this incident involving President Spencer W. Kimball. A young man going to school at BYU–Hawaii ignored suggestions that he should go on a mission. To demonstrate his rebellious attitude, he grew his hair long in violation of the school's dress code. When it would come time to go to class, he would tuck his hair under a baseball cap. One day he was sitting outside of the temple, lost in thought, when he noticed a group of people gathering by the entrance. At that moment, President Kimball appeared among the group. The young man was concerned that President Kimball would see him and discern his bad attitude and reprove him for having long hair. As the group came closer to him, the prophet left the group and walked directly to him. The young man said:

> A feeling of shame engulfed my soul and I wanted to run. When he reached me, he threw his arms around my neck, kissed my cheek, and whispered, "I love you." I could not dispute it—he loved me. I actually felt it. I cried. I couldn't control myself. I went behind the temple and continued

> to sob as his pure love melted away my anger and bitterness.[3]

As in the above example, you are counseled to "succor the weak, lift up the hands which hang down, and strengthen the feeble knees" (D&C 81:5). In his closing remarks in the October 1996 general conference, President Hinckley emphasized such counsel to the Saints and related another example from President Spencer W. Kimball's life:

> We have some of our own who cry out in pain and suffering and loneliness and fear. Ours is a great and solemn duty to reach out and help them, to lift them, to feed them if they are hungry, to nurture their spirits if they thirst for truth and righteousness. . . . My brethren and sisters, I would hope, I would pray, that each of us . . . would resolve to seek those who need help, who are in desperate and difficult circumstances, and *lift them in the spirit of love* into the embrace of the Church, where strong hands and loving hearts will warm them, comfort them, sustain them, and put them on the way of happy and productive lives.[4]

A young mother told a story that illustrates what President Hinckley is saying. The setting was a long line at an airport, and the mother could not hold her crying child for medical reasons. Others in the line were critical of her actions. The woman then relates that:

> Someone came towards us and with a kindly smile said, "Is there something I could do to help

> you?" With a grateful sigh, I accepted his offer. He lifted my sobbing little daughter from the cold floor and lovingly held her to him while he patted her gently on the back. He asked if she could chew a piece of gum. When she was settled down, he carried her with him and said something kindly to the others in the line ahead of me, about how I needed their help . . . then he went up to the ticket counter and made arrangements with the clerk for me to be put on a flight leaving shortly. He walked with us to a bench, where we chatted a moment, until he was assured that I would be fine. He went on his way.[5]

It was about a week later that the woman saw a picture of him and recognized him as the one who had helped her in the airport. Over twenty years later, President Kimball received this letter:

> Dear President Kimball, I am a student at BYU. I have just returned from my mission in Munich, West Germany. . . . I was sitting in Priesthood meeting last week, when a story was told of a loving service which you performed some twenty-one years ago in the Chicago airport. The story told how you met a young pregnant mother with a young screaming child . . . waiting in a long line for her tickets. She was threatening miscarriage and therefore couldn't lift her child to comfort her. . . . You comforted the crying child, and explained the dilemma to the other passengers in line. This act of love took the strain and tension off of my mother. I was born a few months later

> in Flint, Michigan. I just wanted to thank you for your love. Thank you for your example.[5]

When you lift your heart and soul to God, He will lift you to Him, and with a new understanding of His love, you will be able to lift others in ways you would not have previously been able to do. Often, you will not know the end results of these efforts, and it is not necessary that you do. But there will be times, as with President Kimball, when years later you will learn how a small act of kindness was a major factor for blessing someone's life. Lift your soul to God, He will lift you to Him, and then with His love in your heart, you will lift those around you.

Additional Scriptures to Study

1 Cor. 6:14
2 Cor. 4:14
D&C 52:44

Chapter 14

The Binding Strength of a Covenant

Whether or not you choose to keep your covenant to always remember Him, He always remembers you.[1]

—*Henry B. Eyring*

Some years ago, a young woman in our ward was disfellowshipped from the Church. Among the loss of her privileges, one loss she said that seemed to hurt the most was watching the sacrament tray pass by and not being able to partake. She did not care if other people noticed her not taking the sacrament. She did not care what they thought. What concerned her were the questions that continually ran through her mind: Had she removed herself so far from the Lord that He had forgotten her? Was the absence of the Holy Ghost a sign that the Lord had turned His attention from her? As she tried to turn back to Him, would He turn back to her? Could she ever be on equal footing again with the other brothers and sisters in the ward?

Some time later, it was deeply moving to watch her joy as she worthily partook of the sacrament once again. The peace and assurance that marked her countenance also indicated that she had the answers to her questions: God still loved her, He had not forgotten her, and, in fact, had been there all along.

God's love for you will never fail; it will never cease. He has never and will never forget you. Through Isaiah, the Lord tells Israel that in spite of all their sins, all of their wanderings, all of their worshipping of false gods, "his hand is stretched out still" (2 Ne. 19:12). And in 1 Nephi we read, "But, behold, Zion hath said: The Lord hath forsaken me, and my Lord hath forgotten me—but he will show that he hath not. For can a woman forget her sucking child, that she should not have compassion on the son of her womb? Yea, they may forget, yet will I not forget thee, O house of Israel. Behold, I have graven thee upon the palms of my hands; thy walls are continually before me" (1 Ne. 21:14–16).

One of the best evidences that God is continually mindful of you is found in the covenants associated with the sacrament. Each week, the cleansing that came with your baptism is renewed and continued. As you symbolically partake of His body and blood, the Lord remembers you by blessing you with the sanctifying process of this ordinance. However, this remembering is not meant to be one-sided but is to be complemented by a remembering on your part.

The taking of the sacrament is remarkable because the Savior actively becomes involved in your life through the blessings of the Atonement, and you become involved with Him through your repentance. Experiencing this communion will lead you to say, as Jacob did, "My soul delighteth in the covenants of the Lord . . . yea, my soul delighteth in his grace, and in his justice, and power, and mercy in the great and eternal plan of deliverance from death" (2 Ne. 11:5).

In the scriptures, you are counseled to remember a number of things, such as keeping the commandments, your heritage (see Hel. 5:6), your families (see Jacob 3:10), the Lord's promises (see 2 Ne. 29:2), and the awfulness of sin (see 2 Ne. 9:39). You're told to remember the scriptures and accept the truthfulness of the words of the prophets (see Mosiah 1:6), as well as exhorted regarding many other things.

But the primary thing you are to remember is the sacrifice of the Lord in your behalf. "Remember the worth of [your soul] is great in the sight of God; For, behold, the Lord your Redeemer suffered death in the flesh; wherefore he suffered the pain of all men, that all men might repent and come unto him. And he hath risen again from the dead, that he might bring all men unto him, on conditions of repentance" (D&C 18:10–12). So you are always to remember.

The kind of remembering the scriptures urge needs to go beyond taking the sacrament on Sunday. It shouldn't be a Sunday-only activity, but one that continues through each day of the week. There are times when contemplating your covenants and meditating on the Savior's Atonement can be a challenge. The world is always going to do its best to get in the way. Life is noisy and distracting. Life is inconvenient and never operates on your schedule. But that is life. Just remember that the heart can express things in the midst of any circumstance; the Lord can also accomplish anything in any setting.

Too often you may ask the Lord to wait a minute at the very second He's ready to come in and bring a measure of peace and sanity in your life but for the asking. Pausing for just a brief moment to say a prayer like, "Lord, I'm not forgetting you, please don't forget me," can calm your heart and do wonders.

You can remember Him in a number of different ways. Here are five ways to remember. Try to do them at least twice a day. You can mix them or rotate them or just do one, whatever works the best. Or you can create some of your own.

1. Choose a favorite hymn you can hum or sing to yourself in times of stress. For instance, "Oh, May My Soul Commune with Thee."

My favorite line is "And make my turmoil cease" (*Hymns,* 123).

2. Take time, even if it's only five minutes, to have a prayer. If you can schedule a time, that's all the better. Use the prayer to express thanks for the Atonement and ask for its influence in your life.

3. Take five minutes to read from the Gospel of John; 3 Ne. 11–28; D&C 18, 19, or 76; or Moro. 7–10. These chapters are full of inspirational verses that will focus your thoughts on the Savior. Reading just a few verses can change your outlook and calm your soul.

4. Find a quiet spot, sit, close your eyes, and focus on the feelings of your heart regarding the gospel. Keep your mind turned away from the problems of the day. As long as you can, stay in this mode until inspiration enters your mind and/or feelings of peace enter your heart.

5. Purposely do something for someone. Call a friend or relative and see how they are. Cheer them by telling them how much you love them. Send a card and say something similar. If you're at work, walk by someone's desk and be caring and cheerful. If you can, think of someone who's a little down. Take a minute to talk to them and listen. Just being understanding can lift them up a bit.

There is a bond that is created by the Atonement where the Savior binds himself to those with whom He has covenanted. The Savior never forgets His covenant people. He will always remember you, but the blessings will roll forth only as you remember Him. As you do, you will be taught. You will be strengthened and inspired. You will gain peace. And, you will be filled with love.

Additional Scriptures to Study

Deut. 4:29–31
1 Ne. 17:40
D&C 76:5, 9–10

Chapter 15
He Will Heal You

I have . . . reflected much on the power of Christ to heal and bless. It was He who said, "I am come that they might have life, and that they might have it more abundantly" (John 10:10). In a world of sickness and sorrow, of tension and jealousy and greed, there must be much of healing if there is to be life abundant.[1]

–Gordon B. Hinckley

One Sunday as I sat on the stand and looked out on the members of our small branch, I wondered what was going through the minds of those who were burdened in some way. They seemed lost in thought or prayer. Along one side of the chapel sat a sister who was fighting cancer for the second time against unfavorable odds, a middle-aged single man who wondered if he would ever marry and have a family, and another brother, recently moved to the state who, with his doctors, was trying to postpone the failure of his heart and kidneys as long as possible. Only a transplant was going to save his life, and he was without a benefits plan to help pay for it.

In the middle pews sat a young wife who was struggling with a husband who was losing interest in the Church, an elderly widow who had to stand on tired feet all day working to support herself, a sister who was in continual pain from back and health problems, and a father who had changed his life and was now trying to change the life of his teenage son. On the other side sat a new convert—a recent widower—who was serving his second service mission and still grieving the loss of his wife.

Even though these members were in pain, all were patiently enduring their trials, accepting the will of the Lord, and providing a wonderful example of faith for the rest of the ward. Needless to say, our fast and testimony meetings were often a little emotional and very spiritual. Their experiences helped everyone cut through the trivial things of life to those that really mattered. In each person you could see the hand of the Lord in their life, and there was no doubt the Lord was aware of them and walking each step of the way with them.

Everyone, because of mortality, needs the healing influence of the Savior, and not just for serious problems. You need it even in the best of times and the best of health. This mortal existence brings new adversity to someone every day. You may have noticed that you don't get too many perfect days in a row. A new illness, a worry, a fear, feelings of loneliness, depression, or some type of physical or emotional pain seems to loom its head on a regular basis. It may be your own burden or the burden of someone else that you wish you could remove.

The scriptures are full of examples where those who had faith to heal or be healed experienced a miracle. Peter caused the lame man to walk. Nephi raised his brother from the dead. Daniel survived the lion's den. Shadrach, Meshach, and Abed-nego walked in the fiery furnace with the Lord. Saul had his sight restored by the power of the priesthood after having his soul restored by the Lord. Joseph Smith healed numerous people on the banks of the Mississippi.

Miracles happened then, and they happen now. The Master Physician healed the sick, raised the dead, caused the lame to walk, the deaf to hear, and the blind to see, and continues to do so today. He has not ceased to be a God of miracles. He says, "For behold, I am God; and I am a God of miracles; and I will show unto the world that I am the same yesterday, today, and forever" (2 Ne. 27:23).

Ours is not a God of the past. He has not changed from being a God of miracles to one who no longer does them. Moroni said:

> And now, O all ye that have imagined up unto yourselves a god who can do no miracles, I would ask of you, have all these things passed, of which I have spoken? Has the end come yet? Behold I say unto you, Nay; and God has not ceased to be a God miracles.
>
> And who shall say that Jesus Christ did not do many miracles? And there were many mighty miracles wrought by the hands of the apostles.
>
> And if there were miracles wrought then, why has God ceased to be a God of miracles and yet be an unchangeable Being? And behold, I say unto you he changeth not; if so he would cease to be God; and he ceaseth not to be God, and is a God of miracles (Morm. 9:15, 18–19).

Whatever your circumstances are, the Lord can heal you. If He doesn't change your circumstances, it is because He wants to heal you in the way you need it most. In your seeking to be healed, it is important that you do not seek to be healed only of the suffering; the Lord wants you to learn from suffering. Every pain has a purpose; every burden brings strength. The Lord knows you best. He knows your limits. So He knows when to allow a pain or burden to be placed on you and when to lift it. Sometimes the Lord heals miraculously. However, healing doesn't always mean getting rid of the problem or disease, nor is that always the best solution from an eternal perspective.

Elder Dallin H. Oaks commented on this:

> Healing blessings come in many ways, each suited to our individual needs, as known to Him who loves us best. Sometimes a "healing" cures our illness or lifts our burden. But sometimes we are "healed" by being given strength or understanding or patience to bear the burdens placed upon us. . . . The healing power of the Lord Jesus Christ—whether it removes our burdens or strengthens us to endure and live with them . . . is available for every affliction in mortality.[2]

No one goes to the root of things like the Savior. He gets to the very foundation stones of your soul and fortifies them. He reinforces the very nature of your divine being even as He teaches you about it. In the midst of your pain, He will give you hope and increase your faith. He will give you peace so that you know that, in the end, all will be well and right.

So when it is the Lord's will that you must endure a burden of some type, the Savior will heal you in ways that make it possible to bear it. In instances that are catastrophic and involve death or something life-changing, the Savior can and will be your mainstay. You will know He's there and will feel His healing influence. As the hymn promises:

> Fear not, I am with thee; oh, be not dismayed,
> For I am thy God and will still give thee aid.

I'll strengthen thee, help thee, and cause thee to stand . . .
Upheld by my righteous, omnipotent hand.

When through the deep waters I call thee to go,
The rivers of sorrow shall not thee o'erflow,
For I will be with thee, thy troubles to bless . . .
And sanctify to thee thy deepest distress.

The soul that on Jesus hath leaned for repose
I will not, I cannot, desert to his foes;
That soul, though all hell should endeavor to shake . . .
I'll never, no never, no never forsake!
("How Firm a Foundation," *Hymns,* 85).

Among those things that supported the Savior in His suffering, there are four possibilities that are of interest to this discussion and that can support us as we face our own Gethsemanes. One, He was willing to do His Father's will regardless of what it meant for Him. When the burden of the Atonement became so great that even He was astonished, He asked His Father to change it, take Him out of it, and accomplish it some other way. He knew His Father could do anything, so He said, "Father, all things are possible unto thee; take away this cup from me." But above that desire was a stronger one to do as His Father willed: "Nevertheless not what I will, but what thou wilt," He finished (Mark 14:36).

This wasn't just a matter of obedience. It was a matter of trust. He knew and trusted that what His Father wanted Him to go through was necessary, even critical, not only for Him but for all of us. If you can come to know that what you are experiencing is according to God's will, you can get through it as the

Savior did because you will gain faith that there is a divine purpose for your suffering and He will see you through it.

The second thing that assisted the Savior was His love for those whose sins He was suffering for. "Hereby perceive we the love of Christ, because he laid down his life for us" (JST 1 Jn. 3:16). My ward members, in spite of their own suffering, extended themselves to others and were concerned about everyone else's welfare and well-being above their own. They expressed their love and gratitude continually. Their ability to look beyond themselves was a powerful example of the love and suffering emulated by the Savior.

Third, in the height of His suffering, "there appeared an angel unto him from heaven, strengthening him" (Luke 22:43). This angel quite possibly administered to the Savior by the power of the priesthood. Don't hesitate to ask for priesthood blessings. The Lord has set no limit or time boundaries on blessings. You can receive as many as you want and as often as you want. He is waiting to bless you and will use the priesthood and those authorized to administer it. Listen carefully to the blessings that are pronounced upon you and wait and watch patiently for their fulfillment.

And fourth, the Savior knew His Father would consecrate His suffering. The word *consecrate* means "to make sacred." There will be a divine purpose for the suffering. It will not be wasted or in vain. In the end, it will be a blessing to you and to others. He said, "I have finished the work which thou gavest me to do. And now, O Father, glorify thou me with thine own self with the glory which I had with thee before the world was" (John 17:4–5). Whether your burden is lifted in this life or after, you can be assured that God is consecrating your suffering if you will let him. There is a glory prepared for you, because if you endure it well, "God shall exalt thee on high" (D&C 121:8).

God can heal you in the midst of your suffering. Miracles do happen and can happen to you. If the burden is not lifted, do not despair. He will heal you in other, perhaps even more miraculous ways. Sometimes these other ways are of greater importance to you than the removal of your adversity. The promise is that in the end, your "adversity and [your] afflictions shall be but a small moment" (D&C 121:7). "Wherefore, fear not even unto death; for in this world your joy is not full, but in me your joy is full. Therefore, care not for the body, neither the life of the body; but care for the soul, and for the life of the soul. And seek the face of the Lord always, that in patience ye may possess your souls, and ye shall have eternal life" (D&C 101:36–38).

Additional Scriptures to Study

2 Kgs. 20:5
Luke 4:18
3 Ne. 9:13
Ether 12:6
D&C 122:7–9

Chapter 16

Receiving His Countenance

But ye are a chosen generation, a royal priesthood, an holy nation, a peculiar people; that ye should shew forth the praises of him who hath called you out of darkness into his marvellous light (1 Pet. 2:9).

For several hours my two high school friends and I had been traveling on a twisting, winding mountain road near Sequoia National Park in California. Each passing hour increased our uneasy and uncomfortable feelings. We hadn't passed or seen a single car. The trees loomed high above, making the night thick with darkness. And with so many twists and turns, we had to drive at a frustratingly slow speed.

Thinking we'd never see the end of the road's countless switchbacks, we suddenly rounded a turn and out of the darkness appeared a brightly lit tunnel. And it was straight! It went for about a quarter mile, so I pushed the Jeep up to an exhilarating forty-five miles per hour. It felt good to be going so fast, but as we burst out of the tunnel, we hit a wall of blackness. Somewhere in the tunnel, the headlights had gone out. I slammed on the brakes and the Jeep skidded across some loose gravel to a stop.

I opened my door and started to step out, but my foot found nothing but air. We looked out but couldn't see much of anything because of the dark. I turned the engine off and we carefully climbed out of the right side of the Jeep. Once out of the car, a heavy pit of fear formed in the bottom of our stomachs. The Jeep had skidded to a stop so that it rested alongside the edge of a cliff. There were no guard railings or signs indicating the road's sudden change of direction, and had we gone four or five more inches, we would have fallen hundreds of feet to our deaths. A light from something deep in the canyon emphasized just how steep and far it was to the bottom.

We climbed back in. I turned the engine on and the headlights magically blazed to life, flooding the scene in front of us. As carefully as I have ever driven in my life, I turned back onto the road. Twice that night, we came to tunnels. Both tunnels were brightly lit and both times the headlights went out somewhere in the tunnel. The second time, we were ready. I stopped before the end of tunnel, and after checking the headlights, I turned the engine off and on again; sure enough, the lights came back on. Those were the only times in our week-long trip the headlights failed to work. That incident taught me the importance of light in the face of darkness.

If someone were to say to you: "The glory of God is . . ." You would probably follow with the word *intelligence.* And that is where we usually stop. We don't always finish the sentence with, "or, in other words, light and truth," which explains what God's glory or intelligence is (see D&C 93:36). Let's reverse the sentence: "Light and truth, or intelligence, is what God's glory is."

In an earlier verse, these same terms are used to describe man prior to his organization as a spirit. "Man was also in the beginning with God. *Intelligence,* or the *light of truth,* was not created or made, neither indeed can be" (D&C 93:29, emphasis added).

We know nothing more about this, except that intelligence has always existed. Joseph Smith said that "[intelligence] existed from eternity, and will exist to eternity. Anything created cannot be eternal."[1]

In referring to you as an intelligence (or *light of truth,* or *light and truth* as it is used in verse 36), it would appear that light and truth is a natural part of your being, so you are inherently equipped to receive more of it. This helps us understand verses 27 and 28 of section 93: "And no man receiveth a fulness unless he keepeth his commandments. He that keepeth his commandments *receiveth truth and light, until he is glorified in truth* and knoweth all things" (emphasis added). In other words, as you receive light and truth, or intelligence, you are receiving and sharing in a portion of God's glory.

The Savior is our example of this. Notice what the Apostle John says about Him:

> And I, John, bear record that I beheld his glory, as the glory of the Only Begotten of the Father. . . .
>
> And I, John, saw that he received not of the fulness at the first, but received grace for grace;
>
> And he received not of the fulness at the first, but continued from grace to grace, until he received a fulness;
>
> And thus he was called the Son of God, because he received not of the fulness at the first.
>
> And I, John, bear record that *he received a fulness of the glory of the Father;*

> And he received all power, both in heaven and on earth, and the glory of the Father was with him, for he dwelt in him (D&C 93:11–14, 16–17, emphasis added).

Then the Savior speaks to you and says, "I give unto you these sayings that you may understand and know how to worship, and know what you worship, that you may come unto the Father in my name, and in due time receive of his fulness. For if you keep my commandments *you shall receive of his fulness, and be glorified in me as I am in the Father;* therefore, I say unto you, you shall receive grace for grace" (D&C 93:19–20, emphasis added). In other words, as you are righteous and obedient, you receive more light and truth; you grow line upon line until you are glorified with the same glory that glorifies the Father and the Son.

There was no darkness as we drove into the tunnel. Darkness cannot abide the presence of light. The introduction of light, no matter how small, causes darkness to leave. The brighter the light, the farther it flees until there is no perceivable darkness. On the other hand, when we left the light outside the tunnel, it was pitch black. If you allow darkness into your life through disobedience and unbelief, the light will become dimmer and dimmer. One serious warning in the Doctrine and Covenants is, "And he that repents not, from him shall be taken even the light which he has received; for my Spirit shall not always strive with man" (D&C 1:33).

Darkness is described in many foreboding ways in the scriptures, such as the "power of darkness" (Col. 1:13), "chains of darkness" (2 Pet. 2:4), and the "scales of darkness" (2 Ne. 30:6). Darkness can have a powerful, controlling influence. Darkness can also be a trap; as your eyes adjust to the light around you, your brain assumes that whatever light there happens to be is the norm. As darkness increases, your eyes and brain adjust. After a while, you don't notice the difference.

And in terms of spirituality, you don't always notice the difference in how you think and feel. You become blind to the truth. "The light of the body is the eye: if therefore thine eye be single [to God's glory], thy whole body shall be full of light. But if thine eye be evil, thy whole body shall be full of darkness. If therefore the light that is in thee be darkness, how great is that darkness!" (Matt. 6:22–23). If you allow darkness to be present in your life, your countenance will darken also. Perceptive bishops often have the experience of knowing that the person sitting across from them is in a state of sinfulness simply by observing their countenance.

When God said, "Let there be light" (Gen. 1:3), He wasn't just referring to physical light.

He was also referring to the Light of Christ filling the immensity of space. And when He separated the light from the darkness, it wasn't just physical darkness. He was also establishing a division between two domains, one of light that He rules as the "light of the world" (John 8:12), and one of darkness ruled by Satan. You are commanded to separate yourself from all darkness. "Let us therefore cast off the works of darkness, and let us put on the armour of light" (Rom. 13:12).

A match lit in a dark room will cast light around itself. However small the amount of light the match gives off, the darkness has to flee from it. Whatever the level of your light, the important thing is to receive more light by obedience and righteousness. Live your life so that it places you in a position to receive light and truth, to receive knowledge and intelligence, to receive revelation. "Draw near unto me and I will draw near unto you; seek me diligently and ye shall find me; ask, and ye shall receive; knock, and it shall be opened unto you" (D&C 88:63).

Make up your mind to put forth whatever effort is necessary. A simple changing of your mind without an accompanying change of actions will not work. But a change of heart coupled with a change of action will guarantee your receiving more light and truth. As the light increases in you, your countenance will change and reflect His countenance. Because of your spiritual "genes," it is a natural, spiritual process.

As your life is guided by light and truth, your countenance will reflect the light that is in you, and people will be drawn to you because of it. You will naturally yearn for and seek more of it. You will be a force for truth and righteousness wherever you are.

> And the light which shineth, which giveth you light, is through him who enlighteneth your eyes, which is the same light that quickeneth your understandings.
>
> For intelligence cleaveth unto intelligence; wisdom receiveth wisdom; truth embraceth truth . . . light cleaveth unto light. . . .
>
> And if your eye be single to my glory, your whole bodies shall be filled with light, and there shall be no darkness in you; and that body which is filled with light comprehendeth all things (D&C 88:11, 40, 67).

Additional Scriptures to Study

Isa. 60:1–3
John 3:18–21
2 Cor. 4:6
2 Ne. 30:6

Chapter 17

Perfect Love Casteth Out All Fear

> *You gain strength, courage and confidence by every experience in which you really stop to look fear in the face. . . . You must do the thing you think you cannot do.*[1]
>
> —*Eleanor Roosevelt*

Many fears originate from life's experiences, especially those when you were young. Fear can be healthy and alert you to danger and prepare you for action. It can give you a sense that something is wrong before it is apparent. Unhealthy fear stops you from doing normal or insignificant things, and even significant things. It keeps you from being bold, from reaching beyond the safe havens of your life and achieving things great or small. Too often, fear rears its ugly head and says things like, *Don't do that, you'll fail,* or *Don't say anything to them, they'll be offended.*

Fear is the antithesis of faith. So it stands to reason that if faith comes from the Lord, then most fear must come from Satan. God uses faith to bring us closer to Him. Satan uses fear to steer you in his direction. "All of us experience fear now and again," said President Hinckley. "But God has not given us the spirit of fear. That comes from the adversary. When we recognize that, then we can tell the adversary to get behind us, and we can go forward with courage."[2]

I learned the effects of fear on my mission at times—in the lives of other missionaries and especially in the lives of our investigators. Each time, something important was lost to fear. I saw how fear, especially of the unknown, could keep a person from having significant, life-changing experiences.

One day, my mission companion and I rang a doorbell, and the man answering shocked us with the words, "Where have you been? We've been waiting for you." In our hours and hours of tracting, that wasn't what we usually heard from the other side of a door. He invited us in and explained that he and his family had been to the Hill Cumorah Pageant. They had been so touched by the presentation, they had filled out a referral card requesting the missionaries to come to their home. As you can imagine, our hearts started pounding. We looked at each other; the word *golden* was obviously simultaneously streaming through our minds.

He called his wife into the room, and she shared the same enthusiasm with her husband. Not to waste any time, we began teaching them the first lesson. Partway through he suddenly said, "We have to stop." Our hearts sank for a second, and we wondered if they had decided this wasn't what they thought it was going to be. He said he didn't want us to go any further because he wanted his whole family to hear this lesson and asked us to come back that night.

When we returned, we found a family of seven with two of the children already married. Our heads were swimming. The average missionary in our area baptized four people. And here we were sitting in front of nine, all of baptism age, who were accepting everything we taught as fast as we could feed it to them. We were so thrilled to teach them we didn't even mind their soybean hamburgers and tofu potatoes when we had dinner with them. They were excited to learn, and we were excited to teach.

They began attending church, and a baptismal date was set. We completed the lessons, and on a final visit before their baptisms, the family all gathered to meet with us. We were planning to talk about their becoming members of the Church, but instead they told us they could not accept the principle of tithing and so they could not be baptized. They had discussed everything as a family, and the decision was final.

We were heartbroken. Nothing we said could change their minds. We never knew exactly what had happened, but we knew tithing wasn't at the heart of the matter. Where there had been faith, light, and enthusiasm in their faces, we now saw fear, darkness, and doubt. We were never able to learn if their fears of becoming members of the Church were based on anything that could have been easily resolved. But fear had become the driving force in this family.

Fear inhibits everyone in some way. Have you ever lost opportunities to share the gospel because you feared how someone might react? Maybe you told yourself, *I'll wait for the Spirit to direct me* (famous last words with the emphasis on *wait*). You might have been sitting on a plane or a bus, thinking, *The person next me seems nice. I should discuss the gospel with them.* But you don't. Fear and Satan win again. Proverbs 29 says, "The fear of man bringeth a snare" (v. 29). Or as Isaiah says, "Hearken unto me, ye that know righteousness, the people in whose heart I have written my law, fear ye not the reproach of men, neither be ye afraid of their revilings" (2 Ne. 8:7).

If fear stops you from acting, the problem may be one of focus. Author and physician Thom Rutledge said, "The great majority of the emotional distress we experience results from how we think about ourselves and our circumstances, rather than the circumstances themselves."[3] In other words, you may need to stop thinking about yourself in the circumstance you're in and just do what you should do: instead of worrying about how the people on the plane or the bus may react, just act.

Judgment and fear are great companions. It is easy to discount someone or something because you fear them or it. Fear is also a destroyer of love. But the opposite is also true: "Perfect love casteth out all fear" (Moro. 8:16), much like the light dispels darkness. If you want to fulfill God's purpose for your life, let God's love replace your fear. Having love for others enables you to face fear head-on each time it rears its ugly head. Sincere love shifts the emphasis from you to them.

Having experienced God's love does not mean you will be free from fear. As President Henry B. Eyring puts it, "Even having felt that love, the true disciple sometimes feels anxiety. The Apostle John was clear about that: fear will be gone when we are made *perfect* in love. We can pray for that gift of perfect love. We can pray with confidence that we can feel the Savior's love for us and for all we meet. He loved us and them enough to pay the price of all our sins. It is one thing to believe that. It is something far more to have our hearts changed to feel it every moment."[4]

With the gospel, you have much to offer to others. More than at any other time, there is a great need for all people to understand how much God loves them. And through your love, any fear of rejection, reviling, embarrassment, or loss on your part will become far less important to you. Joseph Smith eloquently stated, "Love is one of the chief characteristics of Deity, and ought to be manifested by those who aspire to be the sons of God. A man filled with the love of God, is not content with blessing his family alone, but ranges through the whole world, anxious to bless the whole human race . . . who are candidates for immortality, but strangers to truth."[5]

Be loving and fear will be dispelled. Be bold and fear will not keep you from accomplishing the things you should. When fear comes into your life, do not be afraid to stare it down and cast it aside. Consider the possibilities that are before you and move forward with faith. Whatever the outcome, you will be sure of fulfilling God's purpose for your life.

Additional Scriptures to Study

D&C 30:11
D&C 60:2
D&C 67:3

Chapter 18

Getting Past Your Stumbling Blocks

When the prodigal boy . . . "came to himself," his first words were, "I will arise and go to my father" (Luke 15:18). While he is yet afar off the waiting father sees him coming and is moved with compassion. Repentance is but the homesickness of the soul, and the uninterrupted and watchful care of the parent is the fairest earthly type of the unfailing forgiveness of God.[1]

—*Howard W. Hunter*

Jane (not her real name) was a beautiful twenty-year-old woman. As a new (and relatively young) first counselor in the bishopric, I hadn't sensed anything seriously wrong. Casual observance led me to believe she wasn't as happy as she could be, but she was pleasant to be around. She did tend to stay on the sidelines rather than participate fully in the ward, but she was at church every Sunday. Young people at that age are often unsure of themselves and their testimonies. Perhaps she was too, I'd decided.

Then one day in a bishopric meeting, the bishop announced that a disciplinary council would be held in her behalf. She had always been strong in the Church, but at age sixteen, she'd found herself pregnant. Full of fear, she'd allowed herself to be swayed by her boyfriend to have an abortion so no one would know. For four years she had carried the burden, hidden her pain, and lived with the loneliness of sin's isolation. Whatever the price, she was ready to take the steps necessary to finally be rid of the millstone around her neck.

Jane was much like Olga, a young girl in an old folktale who had committed a very serious sin. As the story goes, Olga confided in her best friend, who recommended she visit the village wise man; the friend offered to go with her for moral support. As they sat in the wise man's hut, he listened patiently as Olga tearfully confessed her sin, and her friend all too eagerly filled in the missing details.

After hearing Olga, the wise man came out with a large sack. He gave it to Olga and told her to find the largest stone that would fit in the sack and then bring it back to him. Seeing the size of the sack and imagining how heavy such a stone would be, Olga burst into tears again, saying she couldn't do it, she didn't have the strength. The wise man assured her she would and sent her on her way.

After she left, the wise man produced another sack exactly the same as Olga's. He gave it to Olga's friend and told her to put as many small stones in her sack that would fit and then bring it back to him. She felt sure of herself. She had never committed a sin like Olga's and thought it would be easy since the stones would be small. Cheerfully, she went on her way.

Some time later, Olga came struggling back with her sack. She was no longer crying but sweating from the effort of moving the large stone. With a sigh of relief and a sense of accomplishment, she set the sack at the foot of the wise man who told her that she needed to return the stone to where she found it and then bring the empty sack back to him. When she had, she would be free from the burden of her sin. Knowing what was now involved, Olga gathered herself and began the return trip.

Not long after, Olga's friend returned with her sack. She was working every bit as hard as Olga had been. The wise man said to her, "You are to return each of the stones to the exact spot where you found it. Olga has always been a good girl, but has committed this one major sin. You, on the other hand, have been accumulating small sins all of your life. You can repent too. But it will be hard for you, just as it has been for Olga, because bad habits are difficult to change. How much better it would have been for you to have sought repentance your whole life."

All of us are prodigals to some extent and need to repent. Repentance is the marvelous and miraculous process of mortality. It is a process of overcoming the world, of bridling your passions (see Alma 38:12), and ridding yourself of any barricades that are in your path of progression. You may have major transgressions. You may have accumulated numerous small sins. Or you may have bad habits that, while not serious or necessarily sinful, can still be damaging to your relationship with the Lord. Whatever your situation, as long as you are in mortality, you will need repentance.

The Greek word for *repentance* is often translated from the word *metanoia,* which means "to change your thinking, your spirit, your direction." In Hebrew, the Old Testament word for *repentance* is *shuwb,* which means "to return to the starting point" or to the Lord. Isaiah states, "Seek ye the Lord while he may be found, call ye upon him while he is near: Let the wicked forsake his way, and the unrighteous man his thoughts: and let him *return* unto the Lord, and he will have mercy upon him; and [return] to our God for he will abundantly pardon" (Isa. 55:6–7, emphasis added).

Olga, her friend, and Jane took the necessary steps to change their spirituality, their way of thinking, their actions, to return to the Lord. Jane spent many months ridding herself of the "stone in her sack," but when it was gone, her countenance beamed, her personality became vibrant. She exuded love and joy to all around her, and she became a wonderful influence for good with everyone in and out of the ward. She was the lamb that was lost and then carried back to the fold on the strong and loving shoulders of the Savior. As Elder Bruce R. McConkie put it, "How marvelous it is that the saints of God have power to cleanse and perfect their souls if they will repent!"[2]

How much you value and apply the principle of repentance to your life is an indication of how much you value and appreciate the Lord's suffering for your sins. The importance of this principle can be seen in the Lord's instructions to missionaries. He says "that the thing which will be of the most worth unto you will be to declare repentance unto this people, that you may bring [return] souls unto me" (D&C 15:6). According to section 18, "How great is his joy in the soul that repenteth! Wherefore, you are called to cry repentance unto this people" (D&C 18:13–14).

"Remember the worth of souls is great in the sight of God" (D&C 18:10). Why? Because He "suffered death in the flesh; wherefore he suffered the pain of all men, that all men might repent and come [return] unto him. And he hath risen again from the dead, that he might bring [return] all men unto him, on *conditions of repentance*" (D&C 18:11–12, emphasis added). Between verses 13 and 21 of section 19, the Lord uses the word *repent* or *repentance* seven times. Three times He says, "I command you to repent," and also commands that we teach repentance. His sacrifice and suffering would be in vain if you did not repent.

If you feel hesitant or frightened to repent of something because it is a major transgression, consider these words of President Gordon B. Hinckley:

> Let me first assure you that if you have made a mistake . . . all is not lost. Memory of that mistake

> will likely linger, but the deed can be forgiven, and you can rise above the past to live a life fully acceptable unto the Lord where there has been repentance. He has promised that He will forgive your sins and remember them no more against you. . . . Possibly some few of you have slipped. To you I would like to say that I assure you that even if this is the case, you have not lost everything. With sincere repentance on your part, the Lord will forgive and those about you will forgive. I hope that you will somehow come to forgive yourselves and put your trust and faith in the Lord, *who will be kind and gracious to you.* Already you have paid a terrible price for your mistakes. They have haunted you day and night. They seem never to leave you. Confess them, if that is necessary, and then get them behind you.[3]

No sin is too big for the Lord. Your desire to repent increases as you realize the joy of a repentant life. It will not always be easy or painless. But the minute you begin, you will feel the effects of the Atonement working on your behalf. "And secondly, he doth require that ye should do as he hath commanded you; for which if ye do, he doth *immediately* bless you" (Mosiah 2:24, emphasis added).

The scriptures are replete with promises to those who repent. For example, Ezekiel states:

> If the wicked will turn from all his sins that he hath committed, and keep all my statutes, and do that which is lawful and right, he shall surely live, he shall not die.

> *All his transgressions that he hath committed, they shall not be mentioned unto him: in his righteousness that he hath done he shall live* (Ezek. 18:21–22, emphasis added).

I like to think of that scriptural promise not only in terms of living eternally in the presence of the Father and the Son, but also living so you feel their presence now.

Where do you start? Take some time and ponder on what barriers are standing in your way. What weaknesses are you allowing to slow your growth? What sins need to be repented of, big or small? Make a list. Grade them according to how seriously they affect your life, placing the most difficult or largest sin, weakness, or habit at the top. Go to work on that one. When it is taken care of, move to the next one on your list.

Eliminating this list is a lifelong process, so be patient. Take the time you need for each item on your list. Allow the process of the Atonement to do its work, and you will increasingly find the Holy Ghost teaching you, comforting you, and guiding you.

Give your burden to the Savior. Let Him carry it. Like Enos, you will know you are forgiven. You will be able to forget about yourself and forgive yourself. You will be receptive to the Lord's will and purposes. You will find that repentance is the most glorious principle of the gospel.

Additional Scriptures to Study

1 Jn. 1:3–10
Alma 34:32–36
D&C 58:42–43
D&C 88:67–68

Chapter 19

Line upon Line

The exaltation and happiness of any community, goes hand in hand with the knowledge possessed by the people, when applied to laudable ends; whereupon we can exclaim like the wise man; righteousness exalteth a nation; for righteousness embraces knowledge and knowledge is power.[1]

—Joseph Smith

Susan and I were sitting in the Tabernacle listening to President Gordon B. Hinckley speak at a celebration of Brigham Young's birthday. We were seated in the balcony, close enough to the speaker's stand that we could look directly down on the prophet as he spoke. I can't remember a thing President Hinckley said that day. I only remember getting an overwhelming perception that what I knew of him did not begin to scratch the surface of who he was and what he knew; I sensed a depth in him beyond what most of us could comprehend.

In that brief moment, I saw that he knew and understood things far beyond what I could comprehend and beyond what everyone in that building would probably ever know in this lifetime. For the rest of the meeting, I pondered on what he must know and how he gained his knowledge.

When it comes to learning, there is what I call the snowball principle. As you begin rolling a snowball across the ground, the size of the snowball begins to increase dramatically. More snow is able to attach itself to the snowball because its surface increases in size; there is more area for the snow to adhere to. As the snowball gets larger, the weight increases as the inner snow becomes more solid and dense.

When you delve into a subject and study it deeply, your ability to learn and understand "snowballs." Your depth of knowledge increases because as you prayerfully study true doctrine, your learning is intensified, heightened, deepened, and enlightened by the Holy Ghost. Joseph McConkie noted something about this principle: "There is a definite relationship between knowing the 'true points of doctrine' and 'having many revelations daily' (Hel. 11:23)."[2]

You can know when the Spirit is teaching you. When you are immersed in studying true doctrine, the Holy Ghost increases your understanding and gives you insights that were not there before. Joseph Smith said:

> A person may profit by noticing the first intimation of the spirit of revelation; for instance, when you feel pure intelligence flowing into you, it may give you sudden strokes of ideas, so that by noticing it, you may find it fulfilled the same day or soon; (i.e.) those things that were presented unto your minds by the Spirit of God and understanding it, you may grow into the principle of revelation, until you become perfect in Christ Jesus.[3]

As you study true doctrine, it seems right, it feels right, and you feel an exhilaration that is both intellectual and spiritual.

The fulfillment may come in understanding something you did not before or understanding it in a way you did not understand it before. You will know it is right. Joseph Smith described it this way:

> This is good doctrine. It tastes good. I can taste the principles of eternal life, and so can you. They are given to me by the revelations of Jesus Christ; and I know that when I tell you these words of eternal life as they are given to me, you taste them, and I know that you believe them. You say honey is sweet, and so do I. I can also taste the spirit of eternal life. I know that it is good; and when I tell you of these things which were given me by inspiration of the Holy Spirit, you are bound to receive them as sweet, and rejoice more and more.[4]

As you study doctrine, remember that Joseph Smith also admonished, "It is not wisdom that [you] should have all knowledge at once presented before [you]; but that [you] should have a little at a time; then [you] can comprehend it."[5] And lastly, Joseph also said, "I could explain a hundred fold more than I ever have of the glories of the kingdoms manifested to me in the vision, were I permitted, and were the people prepared to receive them. The Lord deals with this people as a tender parent with a child, communicating light and intelligence and the knowledge of his ways as they can bear it."[6] So be patient as you add depth to your knowledge of doctrine.

It's not so important that you learn deep doctrine, but that you learn doctrine deeply. Hyrum Smith learned this as he was held back from missionary work and teaching the gospel until he had a better grasp of it. The Lord taught him that he should first study and learn, that if he would seek to increase and deepen what he understood, his desire would lead to power—power in the Spirit to convince people of true doctrine.

> Wait a little longer, until you shall have my word, my rock, my church, and my gospel, that you may know of a surety my doctrine.
>
> Seek not to declare my word, but first seek to obtain my word, and then shall your tongue be loosed; then, if you desire, you shall have my Spirit and my word, yea, the power of God unto the convincing of men.
>
> But now hold your peace; study my word which hath gone forth [the Bible] among the children of men, and also study my word which shall come forth [the Book of Mormon] . . . until you have obtained all which I shall grant unto the children of men in this generation, and *then shall all things be added thereto* (D&C 11:16, 21–22, emphasis added).

Strive to have a contrite, humble heart, an inquiring mind, and a prayerful attitude as you seek to deepen your knowledge of doctrine. Mormon made this observation about Lehi, Laman, and Lemuel: "For he [Lehi] truly spake many great things unto them, which were hard to be understood, save a man should inquire of the Lord; and they being hard in their hearts, therefore they did not look unto the Lord as they ought" (1 Ne. 15:3).

Alma showed the cost of a hard heart like that of Laman and Lemuel, showing not only what was lost, but what could have been gained: "And therefore, he that will harden his heart, the same receiveth the lesser portion of the word; and he that will not harden his heart, to him is given the greater portion of the word, until it is given unto him to know the mysteries of God until he know them in full" (Alma 12:10).

A hard heart fails to perceive truth. And once the ability to perceive spiritual things is lost, the natural man is left to figure out what he cannot understand. The simple truths then seem unintelligent, silly, and naive. "But the natural man receiveth not the things of the Spirit of God: for they are foolishness unto him: neither can he know them, because they are spiritually discerned" (1 Cor. 2:14).

Knowledge of true doctrine can facilitate some great gospel discussions and at the same time end confusion and arguing over points of doctrine that are often inconsequential. Doctrine makes it possible for the Savior's disciples to be one as the Savior prayed they would be in His great intercessory prayer (see John 17). You can see an end to strife over doctrine in the book of Helaman. In a time when there was much contention over points of doctrine, "Nephi and Lehi, and many of their brethren who knew concerning the true points of doctrine, having many revelations daily . . . did preach unto the people, insomuch that they did put an end to their strife in that same year" (Hel. 11:23).

Adding depth to your knowledge of true doctrine brings a deeper understanding of the Savior's Atonement and the plan of salvation. Again, the Prophet Joseph pointed out: "The principle of knowledge is the principle of salvation. This principle can be comprehended by the faithful and diligent; and every one that does not obtain knowledge sufficient to be saved will be condemned. The principle of salvation is given us through the knowledge of Jesus Christ."[7] Nephi said this as he summarized his vision of the tree of life: "Wherefore, they shall come to the knowledge of their Redeemer and the very points of his doctrine, that they may know how to come unto him and be saved" (1 Ne. 15:14).

Adding depth to your doctrine enables you to teach and bear witness to, by the power of the Holy Ghost, the things that you have learned. True doctrine is found in the scriptures, and it is important you be able to teach from them. And as it is with all teaching experiences, you will usually learn more than those you teach. Elder Bruce R. McConkie stated:

> Those who preach by the power of the Holy Ghost use the scriptures as their basic source of knowledge and doctrine. They begin with what the Lord has before revealed to other inspired men. But it is the practice of the Lord to give added knowledge to those upon whose hearts the true meanings and intents of the scriptures have been impressed. Many great doctrinal revelations come to those who preach from the scriptures. When they are in tune with the Infinite, the Lord lets them know, first, the full and complete meaning of the scriptures they are expounding, and then he ofttimes expands their views so that new truths flood in upon them, and they learn added things that those who do not follow such a course can never know.[8]

It is God's desire that "you may be instructed more perfectly in theory, in principle, in doctrine, in the law of the gospel, in all things that pertain unto the kingdom of God, that are expedient for you to understand. That ye may be prepared in all things when I shall send you again to magnify the calling whereunto I have called you, and the mission with which I have commissioned you" (D&C 88:78, 80).

Additional Scriptures to Study

1 Tim. 4:6
2 Tim. 3:16
2 Ne. 28:30
Jacob 7:2
3 Ne. 11:28

Chapter 20
A Life without Guile

More holiness give me, . . .
More strength to o'ercome,
More freedom from earth-stains,
More longing for home.
More fit for the kingdom,
More used would I be,
More blessed and holy—
More, Savior, like thee.
("More Holiness Give Me," Hymns, 131).

When you speak without guile, the words come from your heart; they are sincere, and reflect a deep conviction. When you act without guile, your intentions are genuine; you have no hidden motives, no selfish reasons, only an honest intent to do what you feel is best. And when your thoughts are guileless, they are pure, virtuous, and righteous.

Elder Joseph B. Wirthin stated, "To be without guile is to be free of deceit, cunning, hypocrisy, and dishonesty in thought or action. To beguile is to deceive or lead astray, as Lucifer beguiled Eve in the Garden of Eden. A person without guile is a person of innocence, honest intent, and pure motives, whose life reflects the simple practice of conforming his daily actions to principles of integrity."[1]

Today's world seems to be producing fewer and fewer people who are without guile, people like Edward Partridge, about whom the Lord said, "His heart is pure before me, for he is like unto Nathanael of old, in whom there is no guile" (D&C 41:11). He said the same about George Miller: "My servant George Miller is without guile; he may be trusted because of the integrity of his heart; and for the love which he has to my testimony I, the Lord, love him" (D&C 124:20).

The Lord needs people who are guileless. The lack of morality in today's society, the way people are willing to close their eyes to a little fraud, or a little indiscretion, the lack of civility toward others, the small lies, the attitude that doing something wrong or deceiving is acceptable as long as it doesn't hurt anyone or no one else knows, are all signs of a guile-filled society. Elder Wirthlin continues:

> Of far greater concern than the outward acts of guile are the inner feelings and the attitudes that motivate them. . . . The objective often is to get gain or to profit, regardless of the injury, loss, or damage to others. This attitude is totally contrary to the principles of the gospel. It hinders or thwarts the spiritual progress of anyone afflicted by it. The practice of guile prevents the Holy Ghost from prompting, guiding, and instructing us, leaving us ever more susceptible to the buffetings of Satan.[2]

I have noticed that people who are free from guile seem to be doing five key things, among others, all of which are closely related. You may find other ones that better fit your life, but these five seem to be common. A person without guile:

1. **Lives by the Spirit.**
2. **Has more concern for others than for themselves.**
3. **Has no concern for being more important or holding position or authority over others.**
4. **Has a love for the Savior that is greater than their love for anything or anyone else.**
5. **Has the anchor of hope in their life.**

1. Live by the Spirit. Listening to the still small voice as you go through each day's activities will keep your heart and mind pointed in the right direction. As a result, righteous actions will naturally follow. In 1847, the Prophet Joseph Smith appeared to Brigham Young in a vision. Brigham Young asked Joseph if he had a message for the Saints, and Joseph's whole message was to live by the Spirit. Notice the promises he makes to those who do live by the Spirit and how those promises relate to being guileless.

> Tell the [people] to be humble and faithful and be sure to keep the Spirit of the Lord that it will lead them aright. Be careful and not turn away the still, small voice; *it will teach [you] what to do and where to go; it will yield the fruits of the kingdom.* Tell the [people] to keep their hearts open to conviction, so that when the Holy Ghost comes to them, their hearts will be ready to receive it. They can tell the Spirit of the Lord from all other spirits—*it will whisper peace and joy to their souls; it will take malice, hatred, strife and all evil from their hearts,* and their whole desire will be to do good, bring forth righteousness and build up the kingdom of God."[3]

2. Have more concern for others than for yourself. When you are guileless, you are less concerned about what people do for you and more concerned about what you do for others. The Savior said, "The Son of man came not to be ministered unto, but to minister" (Matt. 20:28). That is a good personal mandate. How much you care about others is measured by your service. Service is never convenient. You will often find that most important things you do in life are also the most inconvenient. Children cry at the most inopportune times. People seem to need your help when you have the least amount of time or energy.

Elder Marvin J. Ashton said, "When the Lord measures an individual, He does not take a tape measure around the person's head to determine his mental capacity, nor his chest to determine his manliness, but He measures the heart as an indicator of the person's capacity and potential to bless others."[4]

3. Have no concern for being more important or holding position or authority over others.

Those who seek position in the Church are seldom satisfied. Seeking position in the Church is akin to being the master of the servant when the instruction is "whosoever will be chief among you, let him be your servant" (Matt. 20:27). In the footnotes, the Greek translation of this verse is, "whosoever *desires to be* chief among you, let him be your servant" (emphasis added). Through serving others, you learn humility.

The prideful are always competitive, always measuring themselves against others. As a result, their success is built on the failure of those around them. Elder Neal A. Maxwell cautioned us about the lack of humility in our culture:

> Power is most safe with those . . . who are not in love with it! A narcissist society, in which each person is busy looking out for number one, can

> build neither brotherhood nor community. Aren't we glad . . . that Jesus did not selfishly look out for number one?[5]

4. Have a love for the Savior that is greater than your love for anything or anyone else. The Lord wants you to "love the Lord thy God with all thy heart, and with all thy soul, and with all thy mind" (Matt. 22:37), and all else after Him. The Savior said this in a number of ways: "He that loveth father or mother more than me is not worthy of me: and he that loveth son or daughter more than me is not worthy of me" (Matt. 10:37), and "He that loveth his life shall lose it" (John 12:25). Alma asks if your priorities are such that you can still feel "to sing the song of redeeming love" (Alma 5:26). Three times, the Savior tested Peter, asking, "Simon, son of Jonas, lovest thou me more than these?" (John 21:15). Prioritizing your love in this way also guarantees you won't "serve two masters" (Matt. 6:24).

Love is the way in which you come to know God. John said, "Love not the world, neither the things that are in the world. If any man love the world, the love of the Father is not in him. For love is of God; and every one that loveth is born of God, and knoweth God. He that loveth not knoweth not God; for God is love" (1 Jn. 2:15; 4:7–8).

5. Have the anchor of hope in your life. Paul states that hope is an "anchor of the soul" (Heb. 6:19). Ether said, "Wherefore, whoso believeth in God might with surety hope for a better world . . . which hope cometh of faith, maketh an anchor to the souls of men, which would make them sure and steadfast, always abounding in good works, being led to glorify God" (Ether 12:4).

Hope allows you to see the bright side of things. It gives you the ability to cut through the fluff and flak that clouds your perception and see the hand of God in your life and the lives of others. The poet Samuel Smiles wrote, "Hope is like the sun, which, as we journey towards it, casts the shadow of our burden behind us. . . . Hope sweetens the memory of experiences well loved. It tempers our troubles to our growth and our strength. It befriends us in dark hours, excites us in bright ones. It lends promise to the future and purpose to the past. It turns discouragement to determination."[6]

Nephi urges you to have a "perfect brightness of hope" (2 Ne. 31:20). Moroni teaches that if there is no hope, there is no faith (see Moro. 7:42). And later he makes this interesting connection regarding the results of having faith and hope: "Wherefore, there must be faith; and if there must be faith there must also be hope; and if there must be hope there must also be charity" (Moro. 10:20). A person of faith is a person who has hope. And a person who has hope is one who possesses charity or the pure love of Christ. The person who possesses charity is a person who is without guile.

Prayerfully seek to eliminate guile if you feel it is intruding in your life. Sincerely strive to follow the Spirit in all you do. Put others ahead of yourself whenever it is appropriate. Don't seek to be better than others or have power over them. Seek to serve them. Let your love for the Savior undergird all of your thoughts and actions. And finally, be positive; be hopeful. See the bright side of things. Hope is essential for keeping things in perspective. When you truly understand your divine purpose, you will live a life free from guile.

Additional Scriptures to Study

Ps. 32:2
John 1:45–51
1 Pet. 3:10

Chapter 21

A Son or Daughter of Christ

Behold, I am he who was prepared from the foundation of the world to redeem my people. Behold, I am Jesus Christ. I am the Father and the Son. In me shall all mankind have life, and that eternally, even they who shall believe on my name; and they shall become my sons and my daughters (Ether 3:14).

Like many of you, I am a product of the missionary program. As I sat in the chapel on the day of my baptism, all kinds of questions were racing through my mind:

"Do you realize what are you doing?"

"Why are you here?"

"Do you really want this?"

"You really don't know it's true, do you?"

If someone would have come in and offered to take me to lunch, I'm afraid I may have said yes. I was nervous and unsure. But with a reassuring elder on each elbow, I went forward on shaky legs of faith and was baptized, given the gift of the Holy Ghost, and confirmed a member of the Church. I was born of the water and of the Spirit. I had become a member of the Church and of a ward family, but I had also become a member of the family of Christ. I had become His son.

There are three elements in your earthly birth that are symbolic of spiritual birth: the water of the womb, the issue of blood from the mother at delivery, and the spirit entering your body and giving it life. Those three elements are also present in your spiritual birth into the family of Christ. When Adam asked why he needed to repent and be baptized, he was told:

> Inasmuch as ye were born into the world by water, and blood, and the spirit, which I have made . . . even so ye must be born again into the kingdom of heaven, of water, and of the Spirit, and be cleansed by blood, even the blood of mine Only Begotten. . . .
>
> For by the water [baptism] ye keep the commandment; by the Spirit [the gift of the Holy Ghost] ye are justified, and by the blood [atoning blood of Christ] ye are sanctified (Moses 6:59–60).

After Adam was baptized, the Lord announced, "Behold, thou art one in me, a son of God; and thus may all become my sons [and daughters]" (Moses 6:68). This adoption into the family of Christ came by covenant making.

When the people of King Benjamin entered into their covenant to do the Lord's will, King Benjamin taught them, "And now, because of the covenant which ye have made ye shall be called the children of Christ, his sons, and his daughters; for behold, this day he hath spiritually begotten you; . . . therefore, ye are born of him and have become his sons and his daughters" (Mosiah 5:7).

In Romans, Paul says, "For as many as are led by the Spirit of God, they are the sons [and daughters] of God. For ye have not received the spirit of bondage again to fear; but ye have received the Spirit of adoption, whereby we cry, Abba, Father. The Spirit itself beareth witness with our spirit, that we are the children of God: And if children, then heirs; heirs of God, and joint-heirs with Christ; if so be that we suffer with him, that we may be also glorified together" (Rom. 8:14–17).

My cousin adopted two children; they were given, and took upon themselves, his name. When you are adopted into the family of Christ and become His son or daughter, you take upon yourself His name, the name of Christ. You become a Christian. The dictionary indicates that the suffix *ian* means "related to" or "belonging to." In this sense, Christ becomes your Father.

Being baptized and becoming a part of His family places you in a more intimate and meaningful relationship with God. Each week you can refresh that relationship through the sacrament by renewing your baptismal covenants. Your adoption into the family of Christ is reaffirmed as you promise once again to accept His name and take it upon yourself.

The sacrament is a reminder that you have been buried in the water as He was buried in the tomb. "Therefore we are buried with him by baptism into death: that like as Christ was raised up from the dead by the glory of the Father, even so we also should walk in newness of life. For if we have been planted together in the likeness of his death, we shall be also in the likeness of his resurrection. Likewise reckon ye also yourselves to be dead indeed unto sin, but alive unto God through Jesus Christ our Lord" (Rom. 6:4–5, 11).

Finally, sons or daughters ideally seek to honor the name of their parents, and in a similar manner, you honor the name of Christ by seeking His attributes. True believers "walk not after the flesh, but after the Spirit. . . . For they that are after the flesh do mind the things of the flesh; but they that are after the Spirit the things of the Spirit" (Rom. 8:1, 5). To follow the ways of the world is to follow the way of the flesh. But to be born again, converted, and thus become a son or daughter of Christ is to follow the way of the Spirit. "For to be carnally minded is death; but to be spiritually minded is life and peace" (Rom. 8:6).

It is a wonderful thing to consider that you are a son or daughter of Christ. You become more familiar with Him, closer to Him. You can approach Him knowing He is not only your God and Savior, but He is also your friend and someone whose presence you can enter. The promise is true: "Behold, I am Jesus Christ. I am the Father and the Son. In me shall all mankind have life, and that eternally, even they who shall believe on my name; and they shall become my sons and my daughters" (Ether 3:14).

Additional Scriptures to Study

2 Cor. 6:17–18
Gal. 4:4–7
2 Ne. 31:13
Mosiah 5:8–13
Mosiah 26:18
Alma 5:38

Chapter 22
Finding Your Niche in the Church

All through our lives we should be preparing ourselves with a combination of the characteristics essential to filling our niche in life.[1]

—N. Eldon Tanner

Your niche is where you feel you belong. The word *niche* means a "nook or cranny," a "corner or cubbyhole." Another meaning for *niche* is an "ideal position to be in." Finding your niche in the Church may mean finding the spot where you feel secure and comfortable. It may be a calling. It may be the back row in the chapel's overflow where you can slip in and out. It might be a group of friends in your ward.

Everyone in the Church should feel they belong there, that they are a valued part of it. And yet, so many feel like strangers in their own ward. What a shame this is. You may feel like you haven't found your niche in the Church. It's not that you don't believe or have a testimony; you just don't feel like you belong in your ward or stake. You may feel you are always passed over for callings as you watch others sustained to positions you have never had the opportunity to fill. You see no reason to attend Relief Society or priesthood, as it's always the same people who teach, the same people who comment, and the circle never quite opens up enough to include you. Or your ward may be so large you feel lost in it, and as you sit in sacrament meeting surrounded by hundreds of people, you still feel alone. You feel like a stranger among a group of friends.

These feelings are real and not uncommon. If you have similar feelings, you must remember that God has not forgotten you. He knows where you are and what you're feeling. And somewhere in your branch, ward, or stake, there is someone who needs you. No one else will be better for them than you. Even though you may not seem to have a niche in the Church, there is someone you are probably helping right now and don't even realize it. Someone you have said hello to or smiled at or talked to briefly has been thankful that at least you took the time to include them.

Being a person who shows care, concern, or interest in someone may be the most important niche in the Church. You may not even know who it is you've helped, and you would probably be surprised who it is. The important thing is, you are needed. I can remember a Relief Society president isolated by her calling because everyone else assumed she was on top of things. She was surrounded by the sisters, and it seemed obvious she was loved and cared for by everyone. But she actually felt quite lonely and in need of a friend, just one person she could sit down with and talk to. A caring thought and a show of concern by a sister buoyed her up, and that sister eventually became her friend.

There is no calling designated for these important actions. There was no real plan of action on the part of the sister. It just turned out that a quiet word and a little show of friendliness made all the difference. Many of the most important things done in the Church are quiet acts of service done without the knowledge of others.

No one knows how many acts of kindness and healing the Savior did. When He healed someone, He would often say, "See thou tell no man," or something similar (Matt. 8:4). His gifts were given quietly, usually in the presence of only a few. Most passersby probably didn't notice what was happening. If there were too many around who were curious, the Savior moved things to a more private setting. Even His greatest works, where He gave His greatest gifts, were done with few present. He was alone in the Garden during His suffering. His Resurrection was known by only one at first, and then by just a few thereafter.

We all have a need to belong to something or to someone, and these quiet acts are the strongest evidence that we belong to each other. As Elder Robert D. Hales said:

> We all belong to a community of Saints, we all need each other, and we are all working toward the same goal. Any one of us could isolate ourselves from this ward family on the basis of our differences. But we must not shut ourselves out or isolate ourselves from opportunities because of the differences we perceive in ourselves. Instead, let us share our gifts and talents with others, bringing brightness of hope and joy to them, and in so doing lift our own spirits.[2]

For others, a niche in the Church might be a calling you love, the one you enjoy the most and where you feel your talents are best utilized. Usually when you find your niche in a calling, it is where you want to be and where you would like to stay. But Church callings also have the purpose of providing opportunities for spiritual growth. You know the pattern: just about the time you really understand how to fulfill your calling, you're called to something else. Usually that point of comfort means you have reached the needed point of more spiritual growth and it's time to find a new niche.

A new niche never comes without some opposition. When you get a new calling, this opposition may be in the form of self-doubt, a lack of experience, or a very real fear of the responsibility. Sister Coleen K. Menlove said that when President Hinckley called her to be the Primary general president, she felt an intense fear:

> I wondered, "How could this be possible?" I had to work hard to replace fear with faith. In fact, the first question I was asked by President Hinckley was, "How is your faith?" I felt his question was preparing me to know that faith would be important in the days to come. Faith would be needed to remove fear. I needed to be reminded that all things are possible with the Lord. . . . Isn't it wonderful that Heavenly Father loves us so much that He calls us to serve in ways which give us opportunities to replace fear with faith and to grow spiritually?[3]

Whatever your feelings, you have the promise you will not be left alone. President Henry B. Eyring gave the following counsel:

> There will be times when you will feel overwhelmed. One of the ways you will be attacked is with the feeling that you are inadequate. Well, you are inadequate to answer a call to represent God with only your own powers. But you have access to more than your natural capacities, and you do not work alone. The Lord will magnify what you say and what you do in the eyes of the people you serve. . . . What you say and do will carry hope

> and give direction to people far beyond your natural abilities and your own understanding.[4]

Whether you find your niche in your actions as an individual or in your individual actions as part of a calling, the Lord will help you because you are blessing and healing His children. As you seek to bless the lives of others, He will bring into action spiritual gifts you have, or He will bestow ones you need. Joseph Smith said, "If you will obey the gospel with honest hearts, I promise you in the name of the Lord that the gifts as promised by our Savior will follow you."[5]

In a calling or out, the quiet actions of concern and care are the most important events in God's work. You will often be unaware that you are being led to other people and other places where you will make a difference. For example, Elder Neal A. Maxwell pointed out that "whatever the immediate economic reasons the Joseph Smith Sr. family had for moving from New England to upstate New York, they were being led—unawares—to sacred plates, buried in Cumorah's Hill, waiting to become 'another testament of Christ' for 'as long as the earth shall stand' (2 Ne. 25:22)."[6] Even now you are being led through sacred experiences, the results of which may only come to light years from now. You are making a difference. So regardless of where you may be in the Church at this time, this is one niche where you belong.

Additional Scriptures to Study

Matt. 25:34–40

Mosiah 2:15–18

Mosiah 18:8–10

Chapter 23
Dealing with Offense

> *Believing that another person offended us is fundamentally false. To be offended is a* choice *we make; it is not a* condition *inflicted or imposed upon us by someone or something else.*[1]
>
> *—David A. Bednar*

There's an old adage that if a snake bites you, you have two choices. One, you can try to get even and chase the snake and beat it to death while the poison works at destroying your body, or you can forget the snake and get immediate treatment to counteract the poison before it harms or kills you.

When you have been offended, whether the other person is right or wrong, one of the best things you can do is to let it go. Unfortunately, there are times when those who hurt and offend do not have pure motives, but purposely seek to do harm. In these cases, you cannot control their misuse of agency. You can only pity the state of their heart, but you must still let the snake go.

In serious situations, you may want to seek counsel or direction from a higher authority. In such cases, it may be important, even essential, that appropriate action be taken. But once the counsel has been given and the action has been taken, you need to leave it alone—forget *chasing* the snake, or the poison of bitterness will ruin your life and your relationships. It will affect your testimony and cause you to lose the Spirit. President Boyd K. Packer tells a story of a man who learned this lesson:

> The night the baby was to be born there were complications. The only doctor was somewhere in the countryside tending to the sick. They were not able to find him. After many hours of labor the condition of the mother-to-be became desperate. Finally the doctor arrived. He sensed the emergency, acted quickly, and soon had things in order. The baby was born and the crisis, it appeared, was over. Some days later the young mother died from the very infection that the doctor had been treating at the other home that night.
>
> My friend's world was shattered. . . . He had lost his wife, his sweetheart. He had no way to take care of a tiny baby and at once tend to his work. As the weeks wore on his grief festered. "That doctor should not be allowed to practice," he would say. "He brought that infection to my wife; if he had been careful she would be alive today." He thought of little else, and in his bitterness he became threatening.
>
> Then one night a knock came at his door. A little youngster said, simply, "Daddy wants you to come over. He wants to talk to you." "Daddy" was the stake president. . . . The counsel from this wise servant was simply: "John, leave it alone. Nothing you do about it will bring her back. Anything you do will make it worse." . . . How

> could he leave it alone? Right was right! A terrible wrong had been committed, and somebody must pay for it.
>
> He struggled in agony to get hold of himself. . . . Finally he determined that whatever else the issues were, he should be obedient. . . . He determined to follow the counsel of that wise spiritual leader. He would leave it alone. . . . "I was an old man," he repeated, "before finally I understood. I would have ruined my life," he said, "and the lives of others." Many times he had thanked the Lord on his knees for a wise spiritual leader who counseled simply, "John, leave it alone."[2]

One person I admire in the scriptures is Pahoran. In chapters 60 and 61 of Alma, Captain Moroni sees his people suffer from lack of food and water, and thousands have been killed or have perished as he has led his troops to battle. In Moroni's mind, much of this has happened because Pahoran (i.e., the government) has been selfishly ignoring his pleas for help. In his epistle to Pahoran, Moroni accuses him of some very terrible things. Before telling Pahoran that he plans to come and cause an insurrection among the people to overthrow Pahoran's unrighteous reign, he accuses Pahoran of:

1. Allowing the people to suffer hunger, thirst and fatigue, even starving to death.
2. Allowing the slaughter of thousands.
3. Sitting in a state of thoughtless stupor and idleness while thousands continued to die.
4. Not realizing the blood of thousands would be on his head due to his neglect.

5. Seeking power and authority over the people.
6. Being a traitor to his country.
7. Transgressing and trampling the laws of God.

These are no small accusations. You can be sympathetic to why Moroni felt as strongly as he did, but Pahoran did not deserve such criticism.

Now, if you were Pahoran, and were in the midst of your own terrible crisis, it would be easy to take offense and to shoot back an epistle to Moroni chastising him for not knowing or caring about what you were going through. But Pahoran does something that tells us what kind of man he is. He sends Moroni a message telling Moroni that he and the government are in the midst of a rebellion and thus have not been able to help Moroni. After informing Moroni of his own precarious state, Pahoran says: "You have censured me, but *it mattereth not; I am not angry, but do rejoice in the greatness of your heart*" (Alma 61:9, emphasis added). He later closes his message calling Moroni his "beloved brother" (Alma 61:21).

Pahoran was able to cut through all of the emotion and turmoil, put aside any feelings of offense, and look into the heart of Moroni. He focused on what really mattered. He obviously valued his relationship with Moroni too much to allow words to have a negative effect on it. Usually, those who offend do not have a full understanding of the situation and are reacting to the little they know, and even that may be incorrect. Regardless of what they do or say, if you can look into their heart and try to gain an understanding of them and a perspective of where they are coming from, much of the offense will be lessened. What would have been a harmful situation can turn into one of healing.

It's odd, but it seems that the people who offend or hurt you the most are members of your family or of the Church. Some take offense as an opportunity to play martyr and isolate themselves, sometimes staying away from Church while surrounding themselves with people who will give them sympathy and support. Such reinforcement is never healing and tends to widen the distance between the people involved in the problem.

Sometimes offense may come from your Church leaders. They will make mistakes, and their actions or lack of action will be hurtful. In such cases, you have to let it go. Callings come and are soon followed by releases, and people grow from their mistakes. But testimonies presumably lost over such incidences reflect a person's lack of foundation in the gospel and in spiritual matters, while also revealing a dependence on people rather than God for strength and guidance.

Most of the time, your leaders will be nothing but helpful. And if you seek their counsel when dealing with negative emotions, they will have wisdom and a broader, clearer perspective to offer. And like the stake president mentioned earlier in the chapter, they will have more wisdom and a broader and clearer perspective. If you heed their counsel, years later, you will understand and be grateful for their wisdom. At such times, following counsel can be critical for healing and resuming a normal and happy life.

There will be times when you simply have to be tolerant of the behavior of others. Some are set in their ways and unlikely to change. If they are offensive to you, rather than be offended, it is more important to be long-suffering and grateful for the insight you have of a better and higher way. Regardless of what others may do, you must stand firm on the rock of your love for the Savior and for all of His children, including those who offend you. Knowing he was going to his death, as Joseph Smith left Nauvoo, he said, "I am going like a lamb to the slaughter; but I am calm as a summer's morning; *I have a conscience void of offense towards God, and towards all men*" (D&C 135:4, emphasis added). He was calm and at peace while vast numbers had persecuted him and his people. He held no malice in his heart as he went to his martyrdom.

When you have been offended, the Lord tells you to go to the person in private and try to reconcile (see D&C 42:88). If reconciliation is not possible, then you are instructed to turn it over to your Church leaders in the case of serious transgressions and harm done to you, but you do not take it "before the world" (D&C 42:89) in gossip or print. You take it to your leaders, leave it with them, and then you leave it alone.

This does not mean that if you offend someone you should wait for him or her to come to you. The high road is always to swallow your pride and make amends. Former counselor in the Relief Society general presidency Anne C. Pingree told a story about this process:

> I remember a time when, without any intent to do so, I offended a sister in my ward. I needed to reconcile this issue, but I must admit that my pride kept me from going to her and asking for her forgiveness. . . . I was sure things would work out on their own. But they didn't. In the stillness of not one night but several, I awoke with a clear realization that I was not taking the course the Lord would want me to take. I was not acting on my faith that His arm of mercy was truly extended towards me—if I would act aright. I prayed for strength and courage, humbled myself, and went to the sister's home and asked for her forgiveness. For us both, it proved to be a sweet, healing experience.[3]

When someone is offensive, the best reaction is that of Pahoran—don't be offended. You can choose to act or to be acted upon. To be acted upon means you give your agency and the control of your life and your emotions to someone else.

Elder David A. Bednar stated:

> You and I cannot control the intentions or behavior of other people. However, we do determine how we will act. Please remember that you and I are agents endowed with moral agency, and we can choose not to be offended. . . . One of the greatest indicators of our own spiritual maturity is revealed in how we respond to the weaknesses, the inexperience, and the potentially offensive actions of others. A thing, an event, or an expression may be offensive, but you and I can choose not to be offended.[4]

In the end, you have several courses of action. You can choose not to be offended in the first place. You can go to the person who offended you and reconcile things with them.

Or, when necessary due to more serious matters, you can take it to the Church authorities and leave it in their hands. In the end, it is always a question of healing, not of getting even or getting retribution. Leave justice in God's hands, where it belongs.

Additional Scriptures to Study

Prov. 18:19
Matt. 18:15–18
Luke 23:34

Chapter 24
When You've Been Away

To those who believe but wish their belief to be strengthened, I urge you to walk in faith and trust in God. Spiritual knowledge always requires an exercise of faith. We acquire a testimony of the principles of the gospel by obediently trying to live them. Said the Savior, "If any man will do his will, he shall know of the doctrine."[1]

—*James E. Faust*

Jim found that coming back into the Church after having been inactive was a difficult road. He had awkward feelings and experiences to deal with. He felt unsure of his beliefs. He wasn't sure he had the strength, or spirituality, or testimony to come back. In some ways, he felt that he wasn't as good as the other members who had stayed active. The excuses he had used to miss church began to seem more valid as he tried to regain his footing on a slippery slope.

For Kathryn, there was social discomfort. She belonged, but she felt separate and alone. She felt that people were ignoring her, making it difficult for her to talk to others. Everyone else seemed to get along, but she would find herself alone in the very place she needed to feel a part of things. And on top of it all, there were still lingering negative feelings from when she had been offended because things had never been resolved as they should have been.

Clay felt his knowledge of the gospel wasn't where it should be. This made it easy to avoid reading the scriptures and other Church books. They didn't seem relevant, and they were hard to understand. He felt that prayer was pointless. He found it hard to feel that he was really communicating with God, that God was listening and cared about what he had to say.

Deep down, Jim, Kathryn, and Clay all felt a need to be active again. They couldn't quite put their finger on why they felt that, but deep down, something was telling each of them they needed to be back in church. They were good people who led good lives. But their feelings and fears created a very real battleground in this war between staying away and coming back.

If you have ever been inactive, you may have had some of the feelings described above. If you haven't been inactive, you should still be able to understand what these good people are going through. In any case, it is as important for the less-active person to reach out to those who are active as it is for the active to reach out to those who are less so.

No one is as far away as they think. When my son was about fourteen years old, he and the other boys in his Scout troop took part in what was called the 50-20. This was a 50-mile hike from This Is the Place Heritage Park in Salt Lake City to a park in downtown Provo. They were supposed to finish the 50 miles in 20 hours or less. They'd start at five p.m. and walk all night and into the next day. Fathers were invited.

I couldn't walk with him at first because of a scheduling conflict. He walked all night with his Scout leader, and I joined him the next morning with about 15 miles left. As we walked down State Street in Orem, we stopped to rest. Sitting on the curb, I looked over at my son, and big tears were rolling down his cheeks. My heart melted. I was very proud of him and told him that if he wanted to stop at this moment, he could, and I would be proud of what he had accomplished. But I also told him that the end of the walk wasn't as far away as it seemed, even though the finish was still miles away. He said he didn't want to stop and stood up and began walking.

When we had about two miles left, he became concerned he wasn't going to make it in the twenty hours. I was beat after only thirteen miles, and he had walked forty-eight. He astounded me when all of a sudden he took off running. Being the old wimp I was, I yelled to him that I would meet him at the finish. The closer he got, the more he knew he could do it. It is that way with coming back into activity. The closer you get to being fully active, the easier it is to be active, and you realize you can do it, that you do belong, and that you have a valuable contribution to make.

When you first come back, members will seem distant because they don't want to call attention to your return and embarrass you. There may be one brainless dolt that will come up and say, "Wow, it's been a long time. I'm surprised the walls haven't caved in." But even that is an attempt, albeit a poor one, to make you feel comfortable.

You may think, *I have a Word of Wisdom problem, and giving up smoking seems impossible.* It's not. And although it may take some time, don't wait until you've kicked the habit before you start coming back. The Lord will help you. It will be hard at times, but it will be worth it, and the satisfaction you will have from changing your life will be wonderful.

Salvation is an individual process. It doesn't matter how much you know compared to others. It doesn't matter how much experience you have compared to others. What matters most is that you know God loves you. He will always leave the rest of the sheep just to find you. When the Savior was on the earth, He didn't spend His time with the good and righteous. He spent His time with those who needed to be healed, teaching those who needed to be taught, helping those who were feeling lost to find their way. Your path is your own. You don't have to walk someone else's. Once on the path of your activity, you will feel the Lord helping you.

One important thing is to not have a hard heart. Amulek fought with his hard heart. "I did harden my heart, for I was called many times and I would not hear; therefore I knew concerning these things, yet I would not know" (Alma 10:6). Soften your heart. Don't be defensive. Here are seven suggestions that may help you in this transition:

1. Don't spend time analyzing and agonizing about why you've been inactive. It doesn't matter. What matters most is your coming back to what, deep down, you know is home.

2. Give it time. It will take a little while to adjust and feel at home. As you develop relationships with some of the members, it will get easier and you will feel more comfortable. And you will realize that you are not any different than anyone else.

3. Pray. Your prayers don't have to include mighty phrases. You just need to say what you're feeling. One of the greatest requests made of the Savior was, "Lord, I believe; help thou mine unbelief" (Mark 9:24). Let the answers to prayer come when they come. At first, you may not recognize the answers. The Lord may test your faith, but He will answer your prayers.

4. Read a basic book on the gospel and a little of the Book of Mormon every day. It may be hard to understand at first, but that will change. Your reading will refresh what you already know but have forgotten. You had a perfect knowledge of the gospel before this life, and the memory of it will come back as you read and study.

5. Don't feel embarrassed to talk to the bishop, a trusted home teacher, or a friend. As you open up to them, you will find there are many who really care and can be a source of support.

6. Accept the imperfections of the members. Each one is fighting a battle of their own, and they may not always respond to you in the manner they should. Members may let you down from time to time, but the Lord never will.

7. And finally, hold your head high. It is a noble and difficult thing you are doing. Many would not have the courage to do what you are doing, and most everyone will have great admiration for your strength and commitment.

The Lord wants and needs you in His fold, and you need Him. The Church needs you and will welcome you. The pleading of the First Presidency in 1985 mirrors the sentiments of all faithful members. In a loving message, they say, "Come back, come back and feast at the table of the Lord, and taste again the sweet and satisfying fruits of fellowship with the Saints. . . . We plead with you. We pray for you. We invite and welcome you with love and appreciation."[2]

Additional Scriptures to Study

Luke 15:3–7
Luke 15:20–24
Moro. 10:3–5

Chapter 25
Seeing from God's Perspective

Latter-day Saints whose eyes are single to God's glory see life from a vastly different perspective than those whose attention is directed elsewhere.[1]
—*Marvin K. Jensen*

How many young boys have pretended they were a great basketball player at the free-throw line in a tied game with no time left on the clock? Or imagined themselves as a quarterback, throwing a winning touchdown pass as time ran out? The fact that athletes *have done* those very things plants the seed of belief in many young minds. Some of those inspired young people grow up and become great athletes who live out similar great moments. They want to reach a defining point of destiny. They visualize themselves in such a role and practice for such a moment, absolutely sure they are meant to be the one who will make it happen.

Everyone has some ambition in them. When you're young, you dream of big accomplishments, but those dreams tend to get lost as the realities of life sink in. Life, for the most part, is pretty ordinary and routine. It can be disappointing when your dreams don't come true. At the same time, you may be selling yourself short because your dreams have you playing in the wrong ball game. You should dream of extraordinary things, but don't forget to dream of the extraordinary things God has in mind for you. By now, it should be sinking in that God can make much more out of your life than you can. And for that to happen, you need to see things from an eternal perspective—from His perspective.

Your greatest accomplishments in life will be similar to those God has accomplished. His work becomes your work. What is God's greatest accomplishment? "For behold, this is my work and my glory—to bring to pass the immortality and eternal life of man" (Moses 1:39). What is the most important thing you can do? "And now, behold, I say unto you, that the thing which will be of the most worth unto you will be to declare repentance unto this people, that you may bring souls unto me, that you may rest with them in the kingdom of my Father" (D&C 15:6). That is God's perspective. In the game of life, nothing can be more important than being the point man in the effort to save a soul.

When God inspires you to help Him save a person, He's not thinking of just that one soul, He's thinking of that soul's family, posterity, and ancestors. As President N. Eldon Tanner put it, "By saving one, we might save a family. We might even save a generation. By losing one, we may lose not only the individual but a family and his posterity."[2]

Elder Charles A. Callis, a member of the Quorum of Twelve, told a story that illustrates the idea. For twenty-five years he presided over the Southern States Mission. One day a home-bound missionary came to see him for an interview prior to being released. Elder Callis asked the young man what he had accomplished. The missionary replied that he hadn't accomplished a thing. President Callis asked him if he had baptized anyone, and the missionary said, "Just one boy, a twelve-year-old boy in the back hollows of Tennessee who was so poor he didn't wear shoes or a tie or a shirt. Just a poor little tenant farmer boy in the back hollows of Tennessee."

Brother Callis said:

> I was so intrigued by that missionary's feeling of failure that I decided to look that boy up the next time I went up into that area, and I found him. By then he had put on shoes. Something had happened. He came [to church] in a shirt and a tie. He was the clerk or secretary of the little branch Sunday School. I watched him through the years. . . . He became the president of the branch. He moved off that little tenant farm on which he and his parents and grandparents had lived and got a piece of ground of his own and made it productive. He became the district president. He finally sold his farm in Tennessee and bought a farm on the Snake River in Idaho and became a prosperous farmer. He married. He had children—sons. Those children married and had sons. . . .
>
> I have just spent a week up in Idaho meeting with all the members of that family that I can find, and I have discovered that as a result of that one baptism by that missionary who came home thinking he had failed, more than 1,100 people have come into the Church.[3]

As you know, saving souls isn't just about missionary work and converts; it's also about saving our children and saving lost sheep—finding those who have wandered. If you became aware that a person you loved was drowning, was lost in the mountains, was hurt in an accident and alone, you would probably spare no effort in trying to save them. It would be the same if someone you knew was sick and needed medication. You would help them to get it and see them through the illness until they were well. From God's perspective, spiritual sickness is one of the worst maladies a person can have in this life.

Everyone suffers in some way. It may be physical, or it may be spiritual. Physical suffering is a part of mortality. You can temper this somewhat by taking good care of your body, but you can never eliminate it. However, spiritual suffering brought on by a lack of repentance can also be optional. Repentance will open the door to healing. The person who is suffering spiritually needs the healing of the Master Physician just as much as those who suffer physically seek a qualified doctor to give needed care and relief. But is it easier, or does it feel more natural to assist someone in getting a physical remedy than providing help in obtaining the needed spiritual healing?

From God's perspective, we are expected to do what He would do. In this case, to give our suffering friends, loved ones, and associates the assurance that, as President James E. Faust said, "there is a sure cure for heartache, disappointment, torment, anguish, and despair"[4] and to help them find Him that "healeth the broken in heart, and bindeth up their wounds" (Ps. 147:3).

When God knows you are suffering, He brings you healing, usually in the form of other people. The greatest memories of service a bishop has are not of his associations with the spiritually healthy, but his associations with those he has helped to heal spiritually. He understands that God's perspective is not to stand idly by in an attitude of judgment that assumes the sinners brought consequences on themselves and must suffer for their actions. He knows that while consequences are being suffered, healing needs to be brought to the afflicted. An attitude of indifference on our part is like an indication of poor bedside manner. Such an attitude results in no one being visited in prison, the adulteress feeling condemned when sent on her way, and the prodigal son seeing no reason to return. This forces our brothers and sisters to experience pain to its ultimate degree instead of allowing mercy to provide comfort for the pain.

To see things in God's perspective is to understand why the Savior said, "They that be whole need not a physician, but they that are sick. . . . I will have mercy . . . for I am not come to call the righteous, but sinners to repentance" (Matt. 9:12–13). From the very beginning of His ministry, "there followed him great multitudes of people" (Matt. 4:25) because He was "healing all manner of sickness and all manner of disease among the people. And his fame went throughout all Syria: and they brought unto him all sick people that were taken with divers diseases and torments . . . and he healed them" (Matt. 4:23–24).

That is what God wants you to do. He wants you to see people and their situations from His perspective, to seek out those who are suffering and help them find the healing the Savior can bring, and to do so without condemnation, but with love. Three times the Savior told Peter to "feed my sheep" (see John 21:15–18). In the Greek translation, the word *feed* means "to tend." This is what God does. He tends to His flock. He watches over and cares for them. He wants you to watch over His flock with His perspective and to care for it with His mercy and love.

Additional Scriptures to Study

1 Sam. 16:7
Prov. 29:18
Isa. 55:8–9
Abr. 3:21–23

Chapter 26
Called of God

> *I confess to you that I am not very comfortable in the calling I have received. . . . If I did not have the absolute conviction that "a man must be called of God" [A of F 1:5] to any office in the Church, I could not serve for one hour in this calling.*[1]
>
> *—James E. Faust*

As a faithful member of the Church, callings will come to you. Accepting those calls is critical to your spiritual growth and to the spiritual growth of others. Fulfilling callings with your heart, mind, might, and strength is challenging, and if you are not careful, you can experience a spiritual "battle fatigue." Being burned out in the Church is a very real thing. When you get stretched thin, it's easy to lose your enthusiasm and excitement. You stay dutiful, but your objectives can dwindle to just getting things done so you can finally get a bit of rest.

It's normal to desire an easier way, especially in meeting the challenges of your callings. At times, the burden can seem to be too great to bear. Even the Savior asked if there wasn't another, easier way for Him to accomplish the Atonement. For Him there wasn't; and often for us there isn't an easier way either. We're given the responsibility, and we have to continue to shoulder the load.

King Benjamin's counsel to "see that all these things are done in wisdom and order; for it is not requisite that a man [or woman] should run faster than he [or she] has strength" (Mosiah 4:27), doesn't seem to apply to life very often. We often yearn for a little order in the chaos of our lives.

You have visiting teaching to do, a whole house to clean, homework to do with the kids later, and now Sister Jones just called and asked you to take dinner to a sister who just had a baby. Don't forget to have some quiet time and read that book you wanted to start. Maybe it will help you prepare your talk for sacrament meeting. Be sure to exercise, and if you work professionally on top of that—well, good luck. What you wouldn't do for two weeks in Hawaii, or maybe just two weeks, alone! And while some of the above may reflect the more extreme days, sometimes it feels like we've been doing it for months that way. I don't believe God wants it that way. Even amid the normal burdens and pressures of life, He wants you to have a quiet oasis of peace and rest too. Somewhere in all of the commotion, He wants you to be able to easily find Him and feel His presence in your life. There is a difference between doing and experiencing, and He wants you to experience.

He doesn't expect you to pull the whole load by yourself, even if the only other possible helping hand is His. During some ideal times in the Book of Mormon, when things were done correctly, everyone was described as being equal and everyone "did all labor, every man according to his strength" (Alma 1:26). What a difference it would make in the Church if everyone pulled their own weight instead of most of the work being done by the same few. Everyone wants to claim the same blessings, to have the same equality, but so many aren't willing to pull their share of the wagon, and that leaves the few struggling with the load.

How do you balance these feelings of being overworked and spread thin with your responsibilities in the Church and home?

Part of the answer comes from the ability to say *no.* When is it appropriate to say no? Is turning down a calling ever the right thing to do? Sometimes it's not the calling you need to say no to; it's burdening yourself with everything everyone else is asking you to do. If you're like most, the word *no* is like a swear word, and if you say it, you're consumed with guilt. Turning people down feels like you're rejecting them, and that's not the kind of person you are. You want to be dependable, reliable, and faithful.

There is a difference between saying no to people and saying no to the Lord. I don't think anyone would consciously say no to the Lord. But I do think He expects you to sometimes say no to other people. Saying yes to everything people ask of you can often mean you will always be the one they ask. They know you will do it, and no one likes to make a lot of phone calls when they can make just one. It could be a great reputation to have, but it could also mean an early death! You must realistically look at what you can and cannot do, and then do all things in "wisdom and order," not running faster than what you have strength for. A loving "I'm sorry, I'd love to help you, but I can't at this time," is very appropriate, especially when it's true. The same principle applies to all areas of your life, work, and associations—especially to yourself. There are many things you feel obligated or pressured to do that are not necessary for your salvation, your family's health, or your happiness. Learn to say no and let go.

A call from the Lord is different. Accepting the calls that come to you from your authorized priesthood leaders, regardless of what they are, is the path to peace and growth in your spiritual development. A good priesthood leader will always learn about your life and your current situation before extending a call to you.

He will want to have as much information as possible before taking the calling to the Lord. Then, with that information, he will ask the Lord if this calling is appropriate for you and if it is what the Lord would have you do at this time. On occasion, he will just know that he is supposed to call you. In either case, the Lord knows you better than anyone else and will not extend a responsibility to you that you cannot handle, because when it comes from the Lord, He will always provide a way for you to magnify the calling (see 1 Ne. 3:7).

With every calling comes opposition, sometimes from sources you least expect. Life will still get hectic, but you will have the peace, help, and assurance to see things through. There will be times of loneliness, especially with callings of heavy responsibility. President Gordon B. Hinckley reminded us:

> The Savior of the world was one who walked alone much of the time. . . . There is no lonelier picture in all of history than that of Jesus upon the cross alone. . . . Joseph Smith was a man of loneliness. The fourteen-year-old boy who came out of the woods on his father's farm was hated and persecuted. . . . In your hearts you carry a testimony of the truth of this work. . . . You may feel lonely at times. That is the price of membership in The Church of Jesus Christ of Latter-day Saints.[2]

The loneliness that you may feel, whether it's from the weight of a calling or just being in the world, will be balanced with an assurance from God that He will not leave you alone. You will receive His help. An assurance will come from Him in a variety of ways and at numerous times that you are doing what He would have you do. If this were not true, there would definitely be times when you would not be able to go on.

Going forward is much easier when you are assured through your own revelation that your call is from God. So it is essential that your well not be empty so water can be drawn from it. Take care of yourself, keep your reservoir of faith filled, because when you are full, you will have something to give without feeling you are being drained dry.

Additional Scriptures to Study
Alma 29:9
D&C 9:14
D&C 84:109–110

Chapter 27

The Transforming Power of Testimony

> *Making a determined and confident public statement of your belief . . . has a powerful effect in strengthening your own convictions. Bearing testimony drives your faith deeper into your soul, and you [will] believe more fervently than before.*[1]
>
> *—Joseph B. Wirthlin*

In fulfilling God's purpose for your life, being willing and able to bear testimony is absolutely necessary. You must be willing to bear it at any time and in any place the Spirit directs you to. In fulfilling God's purposes, you must not be afraid, but must be bold. Testimony that is accompanied by the Holy Ghost teaches, transforms, and solidifies the beliefs of others as well as yourself. It inspires others to action and the achievement of greater faith.

In 2005, a group of music students from Italy came to BYU to study for two weeks. Only one or two of them spoke English. Translators were provided who were returned missionaries from Italian missions. The twenty or so bleary-eyed students from Italy were welcomed their first morning on campus by students and faculty from the School of Music and by Ron Clark, who is head of Hosting Services at BYU.

In welcoming them to BYU, Brother Clark told them how much they were loved, how important the gospel was to everyone at BYU, and how they would feel something they had never felt before. This he said to people he had never met, who had expressed absolutely no interest in the Church. Most didn't know the Church even existed, let alone what it believed in. But the result of each day's contact with Brother Clark, the BYU students and faculty, and the translators, was remarkable. Every night, impromptu meetings were held. Gospel discussions would go on for hours with the translators. Doors would be knocked on in the middle of the night and more questions asked. Principles were taught and testimonies shared. When the students left for home, they all acknowledged that the Spirit had warmed their hearts, and that they had felt and learned things they had never felt or understood before.

There is no better way to transform a person's religious beliefs and understanding than through bearing testimony of the principles of the restored gospel. Parley P. Pratt noted an occasion when Joseph Smith and Sidney Rigdon addressed a large audience in Philadelphia. Sidney Rigdon spoke first, illustrating doctrine in relation to the Bible. The audience did not seem overly moved. Joseph seemed to sense Sidney's failure, especially his failure to bear testimony of the Restoration. Notice the power of Joseph's testimony as Parley perceived it.

> A very large church was opened . . . and about three thousand people assembled to hear [Joseph]. Brother Rigdon spoke first, and dwelt on the Gospel, illustrating his doctrine by the Bible. When he was through, brother Joseph arose like a lion about to roar; and being full of the Holy Ghost, spoke in great power, bearing testimony of the visions he had seen, the ministering of angels which he had enjoyed; and how he had found the plates of the Book of Mormon, and translated

> them by the gift and power of God. He commenced by saying . . . [that] if nobody else had the courage to testify of so glorious a message from Heaven, and of the finding of so glorious a record, he felt to do it in justice to the people, and leave the event with God.[2]

Joseph didn't feel that he was a great speaker. Sidney Rigdon, by revelation, was to be his spokesman, something like Aaron was for Moses. But at this event, Sidney seemed concerned about preaching from the Bible in a way that would help people accept him and the Church. As Robert Millet pointed out: "This was no time to declare a message that any other minister from any other church might deliver. Joseph's was an independent revelation, and his witness an independent witness. The result of Joseph Smith's sermon in Philadelphia? 'The entire congregation were astounded; electrified, as it were, and overwhelmed with the sense of the truth and power by which he spoke, and the wonders which he related. . . . Multitudes were baptized in Philadelphia and in the regions around.'"[3]

Don't you love this picture of Joseph's courage and conviction? How he just stood up without any fear and bore testimony? He wasn't concerned about what people thought of him; he understood the responsibility that rested on him, and the responsibility that rested on each individual member of the audience. Both he and they were hanging in the balance with God, but for different reasons. Joseph recognized his responsibility to bear witness, and having done so, it was now the audience's responsibility to accept what God had delivered to them that day.

Nephi teaches a great principle: "When a man speaketh by the power of the Holy Ghost the power of the Holy Ghost carrieth it unto the hearts of the children of men" (2 Ne 33:1). Notice he did not say "*into* the hearts of the children in of men," because "there are many that harden their hearts against the Holy Spirit, that it hath no place in them; wherefore, they cast many things away" (2 Ne. 33:2). The witness is there, but they don't let it in.

When Sidney spoke, he didn't bear witness of the restored gospel by the power of the Holy Ghost. There was nothing for the Holy Ghost to bear witness of. But when Joseph spoke, the Holy Ghost carried it *unto* the hearts of the people, and it was up to them to accept or reject what he said, to allow it *into* their hearts.

There is a big difference between teaching general religious principles and having the courage to bear testimony of the restoration of the gospel. Joseph F. McConkie relates this experience from his mission:

> I remember a cottage meeting in which a man we were teaching asked about John 4:24, which says, "God is a spirit." My senior companion . . . said, "Yes, it is true that the scriptures say 'God is a spirit,' but they also say 'Man is a spirit.'" That, of course, is true, but the second text is found in Doctrine and Covenants 93:33, not in the Bible. Because the room was crowded, my companion was sitting slightly in front of me. As he gave his answer he put his hand behind his back, where only I could see it, and crossed his fingers. We were both greatly relieved that no one asked the source of his text. After we left that home, my companion . . . said, "Well, we really got away with one in there, didn't we!"
>
> The story is a sad one. Neither my companion nor I understood the message that we had been commissioned to teach. How ironic that we thought we had "cheated" by quoting one of the revelations of

> the Restoration, when in truth those revelations were the very reason the Lord had sent us out as missionaries! . . . [Had we taught from the restored scriptures], the Holy Ghost would have sustained us . . . and it would have opened the door to a meaningful gospel discussion.[4]

Are you hesitant to bear testimony concerning the truths of the Restoration? Does your hesitancy come from a lack of faith in your ability to bear testimony with strength and conviction? Does your hesitancy come from a lack of confidence in the Spirit being there to testify to the truthfulness of what you say? Does your hesitancy reflect a concern for yourself and how you will appear to others, that they might think your views are naive or dumb? Are you afraid to speak to others or speak in front of others? Or, are you hesitant because you are unsure as to whether it is true or not?

I think everyone has hesitated at one time or another. There have certainly been times when I have sat in testimony meeting and had the "should I or shouldn't I?" discussion with myself. But why should anyone be reluctant to bear witness that Jesus Christ and God the Father have appeared to man, that great and marvelous truths have been restored, that the heavens are open and revelations are pouring down from heaven? No other church on earth can offer such wonderful news.

This is probably the most important message since the angels announced the birth of Christ. Maybe this is why the Lord gives this warning: "But with some I am not well pleased, for they will not open their mouths, but they hide *the talent which I have given unto them, because of the fear of man*. Wo unto such, for mine anger is kindled against them" (D&C 60:2, emphasis added).

But if you bear testimony, He makes these two promises: "Nevertheless, ye are blessed, for the testimony which ye have borne is recorded in heaven for the angels to look upon; and they rejoice over you, and your sins are forgiven you" (D&C 62:3). "Behold, I say unto you that it is my will that you should go forth and not tarry, neither be idle but labor with your might— Lifting up your voices as with the sound of a trump, proclaiming the truth according to the revelations and commandments which I have given you. And thus, if ye are faithful ye shall be laden with many sheaves, and crowned with honor, and glory, and immortality, and eternal life" (D&C 75:3–5).

The most effective testimonies are those that are simple. Powerful testimony bearing is not reserved for a special few. It is when someone aspires to be "powerful," or "knowledgeable," or "spiritual," that things fall flat. People who successfully bear witness to the principles of the gospel have learned one important lesson; the truths of the Restoration stand on their own.

You do not have to convince anyone of truth. The Holy Ghost will do that for you. You only have to speak it. It is the other person's responsibility to weigh things in the balance and decide if they are going to let the Holy Ghost touch their heart, choose to listen to it, and then act. I often wonder if I would have pursued my investigation of the Church if Elder Rosvall had not, on numerous times, looked me in the eye and, with the power of the Holy Ghost penetrating my heart, said, "Richard, I know these things are true."

Bearing your testimony will transform the lives of others and it will transform your life. Your testimony will grow in strength and power. You will become more and more accustomed to sharing it. Your desire to share it will grow exponentially as you see the Holy Ghost influence the lives of those you bear witness to. "Wherefore, be of good cheer, and do not fear, for I the Lord am with you, and will stand by you; and ye shall bear record of me, even Jesus Christ, that I am the Son of the living God, that I was, that I am, and that I am to come" (D&C 68:6).

Additional Scriptures to Study

Rom. 10:13–15
Alma 17:2–3
D&C 19:31–32, 37
D&C 33:8–10

Chapter 28

Six Attributes for Success

I do not ask for any crown
But that which all may win;
Nor try to conquer any world
Except the one within.[1]

—Louisa May Alcott

No one who is successful in the true sense of the word is unhappy. There are six attributes that are necessary for your success and happiness. D&C 12:8 says, "And no one can assist in this work except he shall be humble and full of love, having faith, hope, and charity, being temperate in all things, whatsoever shall be entrusted to his care." These six attributes are tools the Lord will give you for your success.

1. Humility. King Benjamin taught that you should "render all the thanks and praise which your whole soul has power to possess, to that God who has created you, and has kept and preserved you, and has caused that ye should rejoice, and has granted that ye should live in peace one with another" (Mosiah 2:20). Never credit yourself for what God has done. Everything you enjoy comes from Him. Listing each night the ways God has blessed you during the day will help you to see His hand in your life. Each morning you will awake knowing that He will be involved in your life that day also. What a great source of comfort this is, even in the most difficult of times. Such humility will help you keep things in perspective and provide the realization that as you meet the challenges of each day, you don't have to meet them alone.

2. Full of love. The two great commandments are to "love the Lord thy God with all thy heart, and with all thy soul, and with all thy mind" and to "love thy neighbour as thyself" (Matt. 22:37, 39). King Benjamin says you should "be filled with love towards God and all men" (Mosiah 2:4). There are no qualifying statements in the scriptures that place limitations on who, when, or how you should love. The Lord says you should love all men and women, even those who "despitefully use you" (Matt. 5:44) and don't really deserve it. "He that saith he is in the light, and hateth his brother, is in darkness even until now. He that loveth his brother abideth in the light, and *there is none occasion of stumbling in him*" (1 Jn. 2:9–10, emphasis added). Each day, pray to love everyone you come in contact with. Pray to be a blessing in someone's life.

3. Faith. President Hinckley said:

> Yes, this work requires sacrifice, it requires effort, it requires courage to speak out and faith to try. This cause does not need critics; it does not need doubters. It needs men and women of solemn purpose. As Paul wrote to Timothy: "God hath not given us the spirit of fear; but of power, and of love, and of a sound mind. Be not thou therefore ashamed of the testimony of our Lord" (2 Tim. 1:7–8). *I wish that every member of this church would put those words where he [or she] might see them every morning as he [or she] begins [the] day.* They would give us the courage to speak up, they would give us the faith to try, they would

> strengthen our conviction of the Lord Jesus Christ. I believe that more miracles would happen over the earth.[2]

That is what the Lord expects of you; to try, to speak up, to not doubt but move forward, knowing that the Lord is there for you, and in the end you will be successful.

4. Hope. No one hopes like a child. They are eternal optimists. A child sees the end regardless of the beginning. Disappointment may intervene, but hope always remains. They see the crop in full growth whether the crop is a new bike, a new day, or a new activity. The Lord wants you to be childlike and be filled with hope. He wants you to move forward with a "steadfastness in Christ, having a perfect brightness of hope" (2 Ne. 31:20). Elder Neal A. Maxwell gave these insights about continuing forward in hope: "Whatever our humble furrow, we are to 'plow in hope' [1 Cor. 9:10]. . . . Those who 'plow in hope' not only understand the law of the harvest but they also understand what growing seasons are all about. True, those with genuine hope may see their proximate circumstances shaken like a kaleidoscope at times, yet with the 'eye of faith' they still see divine design."[3] Prayerfully list the things you hope for and then patiently wait for them, allowing the Lord to determine the time of harvest. In His divine design, the harvest will come when the fruit is at its ripest, will taste its best, and be enjoyed the most.

5. Charity. In this sense, think of charity as benevolence. A giving person is an unselfish person. Be giving, not so much of material things (although this may be an area you may want to consider improving in, such as increasing your fast offering or your humanitarian donations), but rather, on a day-to-day basis, notice ways in which you can give of yourself to others. It will involve some sacrifice of your time, maybe a change in priorities, and possibly the putting off of some planned activity.

President Spencer W. Kimball instructed us:

> Service to others deepens and sweetens this life while we are preparing to live in a better world. It is *by* serving that we *learn how to* serve. When we are engaged in the service of our fellowmen, not only do our deeds assist them, but we put our own problems in a fresher perspective. When we concern ourselves more with others, there is less time to be concerned with ourselves. In the midst of the miracle of serving, there is the promise of Jesus that by losing ourselves, we find ourselves! Not only do we "find" ourselves in terms of acknowledging divine guidance in our lives, but the more we serve our fellowmen in appropriate ways, the more substance there is to our souls. We become more significant individuals as we serve others. We become more substantive as we serve others. Indeed, it is easier to "find" ourselves because there is so much more of us to find![4]

In your journal, list any ways you have given of yourself each day.

6. Being temperate in all things. In the dictionary, there are two meanings to the word *temperate* that apply here. One is to be moderate, keeping your life balanced. The Lord expects you to maintain a healthy balance between temporal and spiritual things. He doesn't expect you to go overboard in any spiritual aspect of your life so that other important things are harmfully neglected. It would be wonderful to pay a fast offering of a thousand dollars each month, but not if your family is going hungry and you can't make the house payment. Another meaning for *temperate* found in the dictionary is to be self-controlled. "Bridle all your passions, that ye may be filled with love" (Alma 38:12). Or as King Benjamin counseled, control your "thoughts, and your words, and your deeds" (Mosiah 4:30). This will keep your life in proper focus. This type of temperance will help you make correct choices. It will also help you recognize when you have not been temperate and how you can address such issues.

These are six godlike attributes worth developing. However, you may want to choose to focus on different ones that are more suitable to your situation. You may want to choose some of those listed in section 4 of the Doctrine and Covenants. Whichever ones you choose, and you don't have to choose all of them at once, faithfully pursue them each day. Your life will be focused on what really matters. This focus will provide a spiritual evaluation you can give yourself on a regular basis. Daily focus will be able to teach others and share with others the experiences you have and bless their lives. It will help you to avoid sinning by doing the things you know you should do. It will provide a true sense of success.

Additional Scriptures to Study

Prov. 15:33
1 Tim. 1:5
2 Pet. 1:4–7
Moro. 8:26

Chapter 29
Finding Peace and Contentment

> *Love is one of the chief characteristics of Deity, and ought to be manifested by those who aspire to be sons of God. A man filled with the love of God, is not content with blessing his family alone, but ranges through the whole world, anxious to bless the whole human race.*[1]
>
> *—Joseph Smith*

A life of peace and contentment comes from being who God wants us to be and doing what God wants us to do. It's a matter of what we think, what we pray, and what we do, because what we think and pray about forms the majority of what we do, and what we do determines who we become. Central to all of this is God's love, knowing He loves us, and learning to love others in a similar way.

Life, for the most part, is fairly routine. It has its challenges and difficulties, but knowing we are on the right path makes it possible for us to enjoy the journey. President Hinckley says he has always enjoyed this quote by Jenkins Lloyd Jones that he clipped out of the *Deseret News* years ago:

> Most putts don't drop. Most beef is tough. Most children grow up to be just people. Most successful

> marriages require a high degree of mutual toleration. Most jobs are more often dull than otherwise. . . . Life is like an old-time rail journey—delays, sidetracks, smoke, dust, cinders and jolts, interspersed only occasionally by beautiful vistas and thrilling bursts of speed. The trick is to thank the Lord for letting you have the ride.[2]

As we make this journey, we should take time to think and ponder about the course of our lives. Meditating on spiritual things on a regular basis will help provide us with a sure sense of direction. It will also help us stay determined to keep our lives on track and to live life the way God intended.

Beginning each day with prayer keeps our spiritual radio tuned to the right station, and we can stay in tune by keeping a prayer in our heart as we go through the day. God is a great listener, and a still, small voice will send signals as clear as the noonday sun to direct, comfort, or inspire us. We must do our part to learn to recognize those moments He is speaking to us. As we do so, we will be able to move forward in faith, knowing that God does answer our prayers and will guide us in all that we do.

As we seek to do good, God's plan will unfold before us. Elder Marion D. Hanks said:

> It is written of Jesus by one who knew and loved him that "he went about doing good" (Acts 10:38). Though from the beginning the shadow of the cross was upon him in all the acts and teachings of his life, yet he spent his time doing kind things, teaching, comforting and restoring, making people happy, taking little thought for his own comfort and convenience or his own concerns. He radiated the deep inner assurances that came with knowing

> who he was and why he was here and what his mission would mean. His disciples received from him not only the sense of his eternal power and godhood, but clear direction about how a child of God should live.[3]

In all that we do, we should seek to have love permeate our life. Fulfilling God's plan for our life would be meaningless if we did not experience His love and in turn love others. God wants us to love Him, and He wants us to learn to love others as He loves us. Being able to love others in the way that God loves us isn't something that we will be able to develop solely on our own. As Moroni states, it is a gift that we should "pray unto the Father with all the energy of heart, that ye may be filled with this love, which *he hath bestowed upon all who are true followers of his Son*, Jesus Christ" (Moro. 7:48, emphasis added).

Have you ever been in someone's presence and felt a love that lingered with you long after the person left? It is a wonderful thing to feel love from another person. Sincere love validates our feelings of worth and gives meaning and purpose to our life. George Albert Smith once spoke of Joseph Smith's love: "Joseph wrapped his arms around me, and squeezed me to his bosom and said, 'George A., I love you as I do my own life.' I felt so affected, I could hardly speak, but replied, 'I hope, Brother Joseph, that my whole life and actions will ever prove my feelings, and the depth of my affection towards you.'"[4]

Many people in today's world seem to have empty bank accounts when it comes to loving others. Many seem unable or unwilling to accept or express love. Christlike love is very different from the way love is portrayed in the world today. Love has been cheapened by the media. And entertainment industries portray love as little more than sexual desire. Wordly love is based on reciprocation—on receiving rather than giving. Christlike love is defined by giving without the expectation of receiving something in return.

Notwithstanding the world's skewed perspective of love, we are surrounded by examples of Christlike love. These gifts of love are unselfish and personal, so they are not often shared with the world. Sometimes we hear of them, but more often than not they go unnoticed, except by the angels and by those involved. Regardless of how widely such acts are known, they are a force for good in the world, and each expression sends ripples out that affect everything and everyone around us. President Kimball gave us the following examples of Christlike love:

> For many years I saw a strong man carry his tiny, emaciated, arthritic wife to meetings and wherever she could go. . . . I think that is pure love. I saw a kindly woman wait on her husband for many years as he deteriorated with muscular dystrophy. She waited on him hand and foot, night and day, when all he could do was to blink his eyes in thanks. I believe that was love. I knew a woman who carried her little, handicapped daughter until the child was too heavy to carry, and then pushed her in a wheelchair for the following years until her death. . . . It seems to me that that was love.[5]

God's love is sure, and we can find peace in the knowledge that He will always love us, regardless of who we are, what we've done, or what we have become. As Paul wrote to the Romans, "I am persuaded, that neither death, nor life, nor angels, nor principalities, nor powers, nor things present, nor things to come, nor height, nor depth, nor any other creature, shall be able to separate us from the love of God, which is in Christ Jesus our

Lord" (Rom. 8:38–39). Christ's love "endureth forever" (Moro. 7:47), said Moroni, and like Lehi, we can know that we are "encircled about eternally in the arms of his love" (2 Ne. 1:15). He will never fail us.

In Lehi's dream of the tree of life, the tree is a representation of God's love. Nephi also refers to the tree of life as a "fountain of living waters" (1 Ne. 11:25). We have been assured by prophets and in the scriptures that these waters will never run dry. They will continually flow to those who will accept these waters. For those who experience few expressions of love in their life, this promise is especially poignant: "For the Lamb which is in the midst of the throne shall feed them, and shall lead them unto living fountains of waters [His love]: and God shall wipe away all tears from their eyes" (Rev. 7:17).

Though we can experience God's love in this life, we also have the wonderful promise that, beyond the veil, we will experience this love in a way that transcends all description. This experience cannot be adequately described; it can only be experienced. Elder Melvin J. Ballard tells of a dream he had in which he experienced just a taste of what awaits each of us:

> I found myself one evening in the dreams of the night in that sacred building, the temple. After a season of prayer and rejoicing I was informed that I should have the privilege of entering into one of those rooms, to meet a glorious Personage, and as I entered the door I saw, seated on a raised platform, the most glorious Being my eyes have ever beheld, or that I ever conceived existed in all the eternal worlds. As I approached to be introduced, he arose and stepped towards me with extended arms, and he smiled as he softly spoke my name. If I shall live to be a million years old, I shall never

> forget that smile. He took me into his arms and kissed me, pressed me to his bosom, and blessed me, until the marrow of my bones seemed to melt! When he had finished, I fell at his feet, and, as I bathed them with my tears and kisses, I saw the prints of the nails in the feet of the Redeemer of the world. The feeling that I had in the presence of him who hath all things in his hands, to have his love, his affection, and his blessing was such that if I ever can receive that of which I had but a foretaste, I would give all that I am, all that I ever hope to be, to feel what I then felt![6]

In order to feel the love of God, we must love Him. We can show this love by striving to live the life God intended for us and by keeping the commandments. As we experience His love, we will know that it will never fail. If we endure to the end, we will live in His presence and experience the fullness of His love forever, the joy of which is incomprehensible in this life. Living in the knowledge of His love will bring us peace and contentment, and our lives will be filled with purpose. Learning God's plan for your life is the greatest discovery of all, and living this plan brings greater fulfillment than anything else.

Additional Scriptures to Study

Isa. 26:3–4
John 14:21
John 14:23
John 15:9
John 16:27
Gal. 5:22
Alma 34:17–27
D&C 19:23

Bibliography

Alcott, Louisa May. *Little Women.* 6th ed. London: Sampson, Low, Marston, Low, and Searle, 1872.

Andrus, Hyrum L. and Helen Mae Andrus, comps. *They Knew the Prophet.* Salt Lake City: Bookcraft, 1974.

Ashton, Marvin J. Conference Report. November 1988.

———. "The Tongue Can Be a Sharp Sword." *Ensign.* May 1992.

Ballard, Melvin J. *Crusader for Righteousness.* Salt Lake City: Bookcraft, 1966.

Bednar, David A. "And Nothing Shall Offend Them." *Ensign.* November 2006.

Benson, Ezra Taft. *Sermons and Writings of President Ezra Taft Benson.* Salt Lake City: The Church of Jesus Christ of Latter-day Saints, 2003.

Dickens, Charles. *A Christmas Carol.* London: Bradbury and Evans, 1858.

Doxey, Roy W. *The Latter-day Prophets and the Doctrine and Covenants.* Salt Lake City: Deseret Book Co., 1963.

Eyring, Henry B. "A Child and a Disciple." *Ensign.* May 2003.

———. "Always Remember Him." *Ensign.* December 2005.

———. "Rise to Your Call." *Ensign.* November 2002.

Faust, James E. "He Healeth the Broken Heart." *Ensign.* July 2005.

———. "Lord, I Believe; Help Thou Mine Unbelief." *Ensign.* November 2003.

———. "Responsibilities of Shepherds." *Ensign.* May 1995.

First Presidency. "An Invitation to Come Back." *Ensign.* March 1986.

Gomes, Peter. *Strength for the Journey.* San Francisco: HarperCollins, 2003.

Grant, Heber J. *Teachings of Presidents of the Church: Heber J. Grant.* Salt Lake City: The Church of Jesus Christ of Latter-day Saints, 2002.

Hales, Robert D. "Belonging to a Ward Family." *Ensign.* March 1996.

Hanks, Marion D. "Failing Never: What the Apostles Teach Us about Love." *Ensign.* September 1975.

Hinckley, Gordon B. "An Ensign to the Nations." *Ensign.* November 1989.

———. "Be Not Afraid, Only Believe." *Ensign.* February 1996.

———. *Discourses of President Gordon B. Hinckley.* 2 vols. Salt Lake City: The Church of Jesus Christ of Latter-day Saints, 2005.

———. "Reach with a Rescuing Hand." *Ensign.* November 1996.

———. "Reaching Down to Lift Another." *Ensign.* November 2001.

———. *Teachings of Gordon B. Hinckley.* Salt Lake City: Deseret Book Co., 1997.

———. "The Healing Power of Christ." *Ensign.* November 1988.

Hunter, Howard W. *The Teachings of Howard W. Hunter.* Edited by Clyde J. Williams. Salt Lake City: Deseret Book Co., 1997.

Jensen, Marvin K. "An Eye Single to the Glory of God." *Ensign.* November 1989.

Jones, Jenkins Lloyd. "Big Rock Candy Mountains." *Deseret News,* June 12, 1973.

Kimball, Edward L. *Lengthen Your Stride.* Salt Lake City: Deseret Book Co., 2005.

Kimball, Edward L. and Andrew E. Kimball Jr. *Spencer W. Kimball.* Salt Lake City: Bookcraft, 1977.

Kimball, Spencer W. "The Abundant Life." *Ensign.* October 1985.

———. *The Teachings of Spencer W. Kimball.* Edited by Edward L. Kimball. Salt Lake City: Bookcraft, 1982.

Ludlow, Daniel H., ed. *Latter-day Prophets Speak.* Salt Lake City: Bookcraft, 1948.

Madsen, Truman G. *Christ and the Inner Life.* 2nd ed. Salt Lake City: Bookcraft, 1978.

Maxwell, Neal A. "Care for the Life of the Soul." *Liahona.* May 2003.

———. *Even as I Am.* Salt Lake City: Deseret Book Co., 1982.

———. "Grounded, Rooted, Established, and Settled." BYU devotional address, September 15, 1981.

———. "Meekness—A Dimension of True Discipleship." *Ensign.* March 1983.

———. "Plow in Hope." *Ensign.* May 2001.

———. "Repent of Selfishness." *Ensign.* May 1999.

———. *The Neal A. Maxwell Quote Book.* Edited by Cory H. Maxwell. Salt Lake City: Bookcraft, 1997.

———. "Willing to Submit." *Ensign.* May 1985.

McConkie, Bruce R. *A New Witness for the Articles of Faith.* Salt Lake City: Deseret Book Co., 1985.

———. *The Promised Messiah.* Salt Lake City: Deseret Book Co., 1978.

———. "The Purifying Power of Gethsemane." *Ensign.* May 1985.

McConkie, Joseph Fielding. *Here We Stand.* Salt Lake City:

Deseret Book Co., 1995.
McConkie, Joseph Fielding and Robert L. Millet. *Doctrinal Commentary on the Book of Mormon.* Salt Lake City: Bookcraft, 1988.
Menlove, Coleen K. "Called to Serve." *Ensign.* September 2004.
Miller, Stanley E., comp. *Especially for Mormons.* 5 vols. Provo, Utah: Kellirae Arts, 1971–87.
Millet, Robert L. *Grace Works.* Salt Lake City: Deseret Book Co., 2003.
———. *Life in Christ.* Salt Lake City: Bookcraft, 1990.
———. "So Glorious a Record." *Ensign.* December 1992.
Nelson, Russell M. "Joy Cometh in the Morning." *Ensign.* November 1986.
Oaks, Dallin H. "He Heals the Heavy Laden." *Ensign.* November 2006.
Okazaki, Chieko N. *Sanctuary.* Salt Lake City: Deseret Book Co., 1997.
Packer, Boyd K. "The Balm of Gilead." *Ensign.* November 1977.
———. "The Edge of the Light." *BYU Today.* March 1991.
———. "Little Children." *Ensign.* November 1986.
Pingree, Anne C. "To Look, Reach, and Come unto Christ." *Ensign.* November 2006.
Pratt, Parley P. *Autobiography of Parley Parker Pratt.* Edited by Parley P. Pratt Jr. Salt Lake City: Deseret Book Co., 1938.
Rutledge, Thom. *Embracing Fear.* San Francisco: HarperCollins, 2002.
Scott, Richard G. "True Friends That Lift." *Ensign.* November 1988.
Shakespeare, William. *The Tragedy of Hamlet, Prince of Denmark.* Edited by Barbara A. Mowat and Paul Wernstine. New York: Washington Square, 1992.
Skinner, Andrew C. *Prophets, Priests, and Kings.* Salt Lake City:

Deseret Book Co., 2005.
Smith, Joseph. *History of the Church of Jesus Christ of Latter-day Saints.* 7 vols. 2nd rev. ed. Edited by B.H. Roberts. Salt Lake City: Deseret Book Co., 1932–51.
———. *Lectures on Faith.* 1985.
———. *Times and Seasons.* August 15, 1842.
———. *Doctrines of Salvation.* 3 vols. Compiled by Bruce R. McConkie. Salt Lake City: Bookcraft, 1954–56.
———. *Gospel Doctrine.* 5th ed. Salt Lake City: Deseret Book Co., 1939.
Snow, Lorenzo. *Biography and Family Record of Lorenzo Snow.* Compiled by Eliza R. Snow Smith. Salt Lake City: Deseret Book Co., 1884.
Tanner, N. Eldon. "Search for the Wanderers." *Ensign*. June 1971.
———. "Worthy of Proper Recommendation." *Ensign.* May 1978.
Thomas, Catherine M. *Selected Writings of Catherine Thomas.* Salt Lake City: Deseret Book Co., 2000.
———. *Spiritual Lightening.* Salt Lake City: Bookcraft, 1966.
Watson, Eldon J., ed. *Manuscript History of Brigham Young 1846–1847.* Salt Lake City: Eldon J. Watson, 1971.
Wirthlin, Joseph B. "Pure Testimony." *Ensign.* November 2000.
———. "The Time to Prepare." *Ensign.* May 1998.
———. "Without Guile." *Ensign.* May 1988.

Endnotes

Introduction

[1] Packer, "Little Children," 16.

[2] Madsen, *Christ and the Inner Life,* viii.

Chapter 1

[1] Maxwell, *The Neal A. Maxwell Quote Book*, 333.

[2] Ibid., 333.

[3] As quoted by Thomas, *Selected Writings of Catherine Thomas,* 16.

Chapter 2

[1] Smith, Joseph F., *Doctrines of Salvation*, 1:6.

[2] Snow, *Biography and Family Record of Lorenzo Snow,* 332–35.

[3] McConkie, Bruce R., *A New Witness for the Articles of Faith,* 512.

[4] Ballard, *Crusader for Righteousness,* 218–19.

[5] Smith, Joseph F. *Gospel Doctrine,* 13.

[6] As quoted by Thomas, *Selected Writings of Catherine Thomas,* 4.

[7] McConkie, Bruce R., *New Witness for the Articles of Faith,* 34.

[8] As quoted by Ludlow, *Latter-day Prophets Speak,* 9.

Chapter 3

[1] Hunter, *The Teachings of Howard W. Hunter,* 12.

[2] Smith, Joseph, *HC,* 6:50.

[3] Maxwell, "Grounded, Rooted, Established, and Settled."

Chapter 4

[1] McConkie, Joseph F., *Doctrinal Commentary on the Book of Mormon,* 159.

[2] Benson, *Sermons and Writings of President Ezra Taft Benson,* 330–31.

Chapter 5

[1] Skinner, *Prophets, Priests, and Kings,* 123.

[2] Hinckley, *Discourses of President Gordon B. Hinckley*, 1:369–70 (emphasis added).

Chapter 6

[1] Dickens, *A Christmas Carol,* 18.

[2] Kimball, Spencer W., *The Teachings of Spencer W. Kimball*, 160.

[3] Smith, Joseph, *HC,* 4:358.

[4] As quoted by Thomas, *Spiritual Lightening*, 26–27.

Chapter 7

[1] Shakespeare, *The Tragedy of Hamlet, Prince of Denmark,* act 1, scene 3, lines 78–80.

[2] Hunter, *The Teachings of Howard W. Hunter,* 92.

[3] Hinckley, *Discourses of President Gordon B. Hinckley,* 2:604.

[4] Smith, Joseph, *HC,* 5:31.

[5] Smith, Joseph, *HC,* 6:58.

[6] Hunter, *The Teachings of Howard W. Hunter,* 90.

Chapter 8

[1] Hunter, *The Teachings of Howard W. Hunter,* 86.

[2] Gomes, *Strength for the Journey,* 302.

[3] As quoted by Kimball, Edward L., *Spencer W. Kimball,* 190–91.

[4] As quoted by Kimball, Edward L., *Lengthen Your Stride,* 5.

[5] Ibid., 419.

[6] Ibid., 417.

[7] Millet, *Grace Works,*109–10.

Chapter 9
[1] Okazaki, *Sanctuary,* 95.
[2] Smith, Joseph, *HC,* 2:12–14.

Chapter 10
[1] Grant, *Teachings of Presidents of the Church: Heber J. Grant,* 181.
[2] Packer, "The Edge of the Light," 22–23.

Chapter 11
[1] Nelson, "Joy Cometh in the Morning," 67.
[2] Maxwell, Neal A. "Meekness—A Dimension of True Discipleship," 70.

Chapter 12
[1] McConkie, Bruce R. "The Purifying Power of Gethsemane," 9.
[2] Millet, *Life in Christ,* 66, 69.
[3] Maxwell, Neal A. "Willing to Submit," 70.
[4] Maxwell, Neal A. *Even as I Am,* 116–19.

Chapter 13
[1] Scott, "True Friends That Lift," 76.
[2] Hinckley, "Reaching Down to Lift Another," 52.
[3] As quoted by Kimball, Edward L., *Lengthen Your Stride,* 433–34.
[4] Hinckley, "Reach with a Rescuing Hand," 85 (emphasis added).
[5] As quoted by Kimball, Edward L., *Lengthen Your Stride*, 446–47.

Chapter 14
[1] Eyring, "Always Remember Him," 7.

Chapter 15
[1] Hinckley, "The Healing Power of Christ," 52.
[2] Oaks, "He Heals the Heavy Laden," 6–9.

Chapter 16

[1] Smith, Joseph, *HC,* 3:387.

Chapter 17

[1] Eleanor Roosevelt, as quoted in Rutledge, *Embracing Fear,* 109.

[2] Hinckley, *Teachings of Gordon B. Hinckley,* 221.

[3] Rutledge, *Embracing Fear,* 28.

[4] Eyring, "A Child and a Disciple," 29.

[5] Smith, Joseph, *HC,* 4:227.

Chapter 18

[1] Hunter, *The Teachings of Howard W. Hunter,* 32.

[2] McConkie, Bruce R., *A New Witness for the Articles of Faith,* 223.

[3] Hinckley, *Teachings of Gordon B. Hinckley,* 380–81 (emphasis added).

Chapter 19

[1] Smith, Joseph, *Times and Seasons.* 3:889.

[2] McConkie, Joseph F., *Doctrinal Commentary on the Book of Mormon,* 3:391.

[3] Smith, Joseph, *HC,* 3:381.

[4] Ibid., 6:312.

[5] Ibid., 5:387.

[6] Ibid., 5:402.

[7] Ibid., 5:387.

[8] McConkie, Bruce R., *The Promised Messiah,* 515–16.

Chapter 20

[1] Wirthlin, "Without Guile," 80.

[2] Ibid.

[3] As quoted by Watson, *Manuscript History of Brigham Young 1846–1847,* 529 (emphasis added).

[4] Ashton, Conference Report, Nov. 1988.

[5] Maxwell, Neal A., "Repent of Selfishness," 23.
[6] As quoted by Miller, *Especially for Mormons,* 2:113.

Chapter 22
[1] Tanner, "Worthy of Proper Recommendation," 42.
[2] Hales, "Belonging to a Ward Family," 15.
[3] Menlove, "Called to Serve," 24–27.
[4] Eyring, "Rise to Your Call," 75.
[5] As quoted by Andrus, *They Knew the Prophet,* 85.
[6] Maxwell, Neal A. "Care for the Life of the Soul," 68–70.

Chapter 23
[1] Bednar, "And Nothing Shall Offend Them," 89–92.
[2] Packer, "The Balm of Gilead," 59.
[3] Pingree, "To Look, Reach, and Come unto Christ," 113–15.
[4] Bednar, "And Nothing Shall Offend Them," 89–92.

Chapter 24
[1] Faust, "Lord, I Believe; Help Thou Mine Unbelief," 19–22.
[2] First Presidency, "An Invitation to Come Back," 88.

Chapter 25
[1] Jensen, "An Eye Single to the Glory of God," 27.
[2] Tanner, "Search for the Wanderers," 59.
[3] As quoted by Hinckley, *Discourses of President Gordon B. Hinckley,* 358–59.
[4] Faust, "He Healeth the Broken Heart," 2.

Chapter 26
[1] Faust, "Responsibilities of Shepherds," 45.
[2] Hinckley, *Discourses of President Gordon B. Hinckley,* 356.

Chapter 27

[1] Wirthlin, "Pure Testimony," 22.

[2] Pratt, *Autobiography of Parley Parker Pratt,* 330.

[3] Millet, "So Glorious a Record," 6.

[4] McConkie, Joseph F., *Here We Stand,* 181–82.

Chapter 28

[1] Alcott, *Little Women,*139.

[2] Hinckley, "Be Not Afraid, Only Believe," 2–5 (emphasis added).

[3] Maxwell, Neal A., "Plow in Hope," 59.

[4] Kimball, Spencer W. "The Abundant Life," 3 (emphasis added).

Chapter 29

[1] Smith, Joseph, *HC,* 4:227.

[2] Jones, "Big Rock Candy Mountains," A4.

[3] Hanks, "Failing Never: What the Apostles Teach Us about Love," 74.

[4] As quoted by Smith, Joseph, *HC,* 5:391.

[5] Kimball, Spencer W., *The Teachings of Spencer W. Kimball,* 245.

[6] As quoted by Doxey, *The Latter-day Prophets and the Doctrine and Covenants,* 3:187.

About the Author

Richard Paul Anderson is an associate professor of music at Brigham Young University, where he has taught for thirty-five years. During that time, he also taught Book of Mormon for five years and Doctrine and Covenants and Church History for ten years. He holds a B.A. from Arizona State University, an M.M. from Northwestern University, and a D.M.A. from the University of Colorado. A convert to the church, he served a mission to the former Cumorah Mission in upstate New York and has since served in numerous positions in the church including first counselor in three bishoprics, Young Men's president, gospel doctrine teacher, bishop, stake high councilman, and branch president at the MTC. At BYU, he is a published composer and has published three textbooks, various articles dealing with group piano instruction, and was a coauthor with Dr. Reid Nibley of a six-volume children's piano method. He married the former Susan Hogan in the St. George Temple, has five children and eight grandchildren. In his spare time he enjoys reading, sports, and hunting for golf balls.